ROCK CLIMBING OREGON

Help Us Keep This Guide Up to Date

Every effort has been made by the authors and editors to make this guide as accurate and useful as possible. However, many things can change after a guide is published—trails are rerouted, regulations change, techniques evolve, facilities come under new management, and so forth.

We would love to hear from you concerning your experiences with this guide and how you feel it could be improved and kept up to date. While we may not be able to respond to all comments and suggestions, we'll take them to heart and we'll also make certain to share them with the authors. Please send your comments and suggestions to the following address:

The Globe Pequot Press
Reader Response/Editorial Department
P.O. Box 480
Guilford, CT 06437

Or you may e-mail us at:

editorial@GlobePequot.com

Thanks for your input, and happy climbing!

ROCK CLIMBING
OREGON

Adam R. Bolf and Benjamin P. Ruef

FALCON GUIDE®

GUILFORD, CONNECTICUT
HELENA, MONTANA
AN IMPRINT OF THE GLOBE PEQUOT PRESS

A FALCON GUIDE®

Maps by Volker Schniepp & IFB © Morris Book Publishing, LLC
Photos by Adam R. Bolf and Benjamin P. Ruef unless otherwise noted
Spine photo © Brand X Pictures
Text design by Casey Shain

Library of Congress Cataloging-in-Publication Data
Bolf, Adam R.
  Rock climbing Oregon / Adam R. Bolf and Benjamin P. Ruef.—1st ed.
    p. cm.
  Includes index.
  ISBN-13: 978-0-7627-4006-2
  ISBN-10: 0-7627-4006-X
  1. Rock climbing—Oregon—Guidebooks. I. Ruef, Benjamin P. II. Title.

 GV199.42.O7B65 2006
 796.52'209795—dc22

                                                              2006007950

Manufactured in the United States of America
First Edition/First Printing

WARNING:

Climbing is a sport where you may be seriously injured or die. Read this before you use this book.

This guidebook is a compilation of unverified information gathered from many different climbers. The authors cannot assure the accuracy of any of the information in this book, including the topos and route descriptions, the difficulty ratings, and the protection ratings. These may be incorrect or misleading, as ratings of climbing difficulty and danger are always subjective and depend on the physical characteristics (for example, height), experience, technical ability, confidence, and physical fitness of the climber who supplied the rating. Additionally, climbers who achieve first ascents sometimes underrate the difficulty or danger of the climbing route. Therefore, be warned that you must exercise your own judgment on where a climbing route goes, its difficulty, and your ability to safely protect yourself from the risks of rock climbing. Examples of some of these risks are: falling due to technical difficulty or due to natural hazards such as holds breaking, falling rock, climbing equipment dropped by other climbers, hazards of weather and lightning, your own equipment failure, and failure or absence of fixed protection.

You should not depend on any information gleaned from this book for your personal safety; your safety depends on your own good judgment, based on experience and a realistic assessment of your climbing ability. If you have any doubt as to your ability to safely climb a route described in this book, do not attempt it.

The following are some ways to make your use of this book safer:

1. Consultation: You should consult with other climbers about the difficulty and danger of a particular climb prior to attempting it. Most local climbers are glad to give advice on routes in their area; we suggest that you contact locals to confirm ratings and safety of particular routes and to obtain firsthand information about a route chosen from this book.

2. Instruction: Most climbing areas have local climbing instructors and guides available. We recommend that you engage an instructor or guide to learn safety techniques and to become familiar with the routes and hazards of the areas described in this book. Even after you are proficient in climbing safely, occasional use of a guide is a safe way to raise your climbing standard and learn advanced techniques.

3. Fixed Protection: Some of the routes in this book may use bolts and pitons that are permanently placed in the rock. Because of variances in the manner of placement, weathering, metal fatigue, the quality of the metal used, and many other factors, these fixed protection pieces should always be considered suspect and should always be backed up by equipment that you place yourself. Never depend on a single piece of fixed protection for your safety, because you never can tell whether it will hold weight.

In some cases, fixed protection may have been removed or is now missing. However, climbers should not always add new pieces of protection unless existing protection is faulty. Existing protection can be tested by an experienced climber and its strength determined. Climbers are strongly encouraged not to add bolts and drilled pitons to a route. They need to climb the route in the style of the first ascent party (or better) or choose a route within their ability—a route to which they do not have to add additional fixed anchors.

Be aware of the following specific potential hazards that could arise in using this book:

1. Incorrect Descriptions of Routes: If you climb a route and you have a doubt as to where it goes, you should not continue unless you are sure that you can go that way safely. Route descriptions and topos in this book could be inaccurate or misleading.

2. Incorrect Difficulty Rating: A route might be more difficult than the rating indicates. Do not be lulled into a false sense of security by the difficulty rating.

3. Incorrect Protection Rating: If you climb a route and you are unable to arrange adequate protection from the risk of falling through the use of fixed pitons or bolts and by placing your own protection devices, do not assume that there is adequate protection available higher just because the route protection rating indicates the route does not have an X or an R rating. Every route is potentially an X (a fall may be deadly) due to the inherent hazards of climbing—including, for example, failure or absence of fixed protection, your own equipment's failure, or improper use of climbing equipment.

There are no warranties, whether expressed or implied, that this guidebook is accurate or that the information contained in it is reliable. There are no warranties of fitness for a particular purpose or that this guide is merchantable. Your use of this book indicates your assumption of the risk that it may contain errors and is an acknowledgment of your own sole responsibility for your climbing safety.

CONTENTS

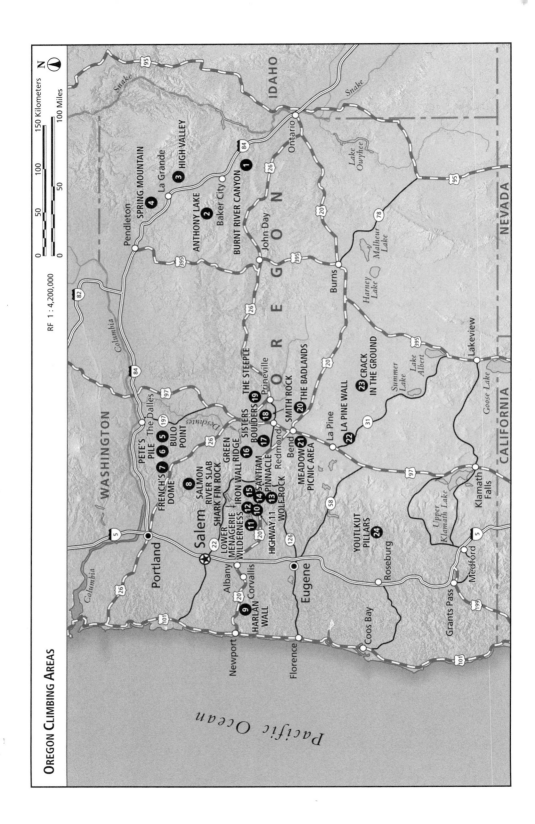

ACKNOWLEDGMENTS

Thank you, God, for the opportunity to write this book and for bringing us down safely from each and every route. Christine, your continued support is a blessing. You have helped every step of the way; thank you. Adam's parents, Bernie and Karen, thanks for the encouragement and for unplugging my Nintendo when I was a child. A special thanks to Ben's dad, Jim; without your influence and guidance we would not be climbing today. Ben's mom, Susan Jordan, thank you for your unconditional love and support. You are truly an inspiration. Brian and Michael, thanks for all of your time, your help, and your support. And thanks for putting off all of that other fun stuff to help us out.

Jack, you were a wonderful editor. Thanks for spending so much time helping us out. You deserve much credit for making this book flow so well, and it was a pleasure to learn from you. Jim Anglin, thanks for the excellent beta on the Menagerie Wilderness. Keep putting up those awesome routes and we will keep climbing them. Steve Brown, what can we say? You are the man. All of Oregon's climbers owe you a debt of gratitude for the years of hard work in developing northeast Oregon. Thanks for the beta and the great climbing.

To our friends and family, thank you all for being such wonderful, loving, supportive people.

Christine cruising up *Sticky Nails* (5.10a) at Anthony Lake.

INTRODUCTION

Known for its diverse crags, Oregon's climbing ranks with the best in the lower forty-eight states. While Smith Rock State Park deservingly attracts a majority of the attention, Oregon hosts a great variety of lesser-known climbing areas that provide a seemingly endless amount of challenging and fun climbing. *Rock Climbing Oregon* is composed of twenty-four of the state's best climbing areas, many of which are well developed and easily accessible. The biggest issue is knowing where they are, and knowing what to expect when you get there. Well, this guidebook is your solution.

From the coast to the Snake River, Oregon is covered in good, solid rock. The state's active volcanic and violent geological past has created and exposed a variety of rock types for the adventurer. The sheer diversity of rock types creates an even greater number of potential climbing adventures. Northeast Oregon claims tall granite peaks and sporty andesite crags. Southeast Oregon hides canyons of bolted limestone and acrobatic volcanic-tuff. Northwest Oregon offers large volcanic domes, pinnacles, and monoliths such as Wolf Rock and the Menagerie Wilderness. The state's southwestern section may provide the greatest variety of all, with columnar basalt, sporty volcanic crags, and even some sandstone. The climbing opportunities in Oregon are tremendous, with crags

Brian warming in the sun on top of an unknown tower in central Oregon.

Ben tops out on *Split Block Hallway,* a 5.9 at Meadow Picnic Area.

scattered across the state. Often, little is known about these areas beyond the local climbing communities. Yet despite their relative serenity, many of these places host phenomenal sport and traditional climbing and bouldering. One just needs to know where to go.

Adventurers have been exploring and climbing Oregon for years. In the beginning one's only choice was to climb in the "backcountry." The early 1900s was the era of the great adventure climber. Loose and mossy peaks posed great challenges and even greater victories for the skillful adventurer. In the mid-1900s the migration to local crags had begun. Local crags, offering improved convenience and safety, became the target of Oregon's climbing population. The invention of the sport route temporarily changed that trend. Smith Rock State Park is often credited with being the birthplace of sport climbing as we know it. Throughout the 1970s and early '80s, as sport climbing's popularity continued to rise, many climbers abandoned the development of their local crags to seek the increased safety and acrobatic thrills sport climbing can provide. Toward the end of the 1980s the sport route had been fully validated by the worldwide climbing community. Local crags were again being developed with new routes to make room for the multitude of new climbers seeking the fun and adventure of this burgeoning sport. Now, Oregon hosts dozens of developed climbing areas.

Within the last decade, an increasing number of climbers have been seeking out additional climbing hot spots within Oregon's borders. Climbers are finding that Oregon does indeed host a significant number of climbing areas—areas that provide the solitude and relaxation we seek, while still offering diverse options of phenomenal, thrilling, challenging, and rewarding climbing. The most popular of these areas is Smith Rock State Park, but that's only the beginning.

The purpose of this guidebook is to allow all climbers to find and enjoy Oregon's best climbing areas. Unlocking the knowledge of the state's crags is healthy for the climbing community, our climbing visitors, and our climbing environments. As the sport grows and environmentally conscious development becomes the norm, more and more climbers are attracted to the challenges of new climbing areas. This ultimately alleviates pressure from the more popular areas and provides greater choices for everyone. This guide provides all the information needed to explore and climb in twenty-four great locations across the state. It is surprising that many of these great climbing areas lie right off roads and highways, but are just overlooked.

While growing up, we spent a good portion of our time exploring and climbing. By our mid-twenties, to our surprise, we had gained in-depth knowledge of excellent climbing areas all over Oregon, some of which were mostly unheard of. After spending years climbing across the western states with no guidebooks, we decided to partially alleviate that problem within our home state. So, we started writing down everything, and a typical day of climbing took on a new meaning. Adding to our standard racks, we were equipped with pens, pencils, paper, cameras, and a laptop or two. Our climbing trips turned into research trips. Days of playing turned into days of work. As suspected, though, we quickly agreed there is no better day of work than at the crag. Formal research and writing started in 2000, and after many years of hard work and stubbornness, the research for this guide was completed.

Determining which areas and routes to include proved to be a difficult task. We had visited and climbed seventy-four different climbing areas in Oregon, but couldn't fit that many in one book. The selection process aimed to include a swath of climbing areas across the state. Those that were chosen had better rock quality, reasonable access, some development, and little or no updated public information. The majority of climbing areas are accessed with twenty-minute or less hikes (the biggest exception is the Menagerie Wilderness). Still, there are so many more phenomenal climbing areas to explore and document. Some of Oregon's best have yet to be developed, and they will have to wait for a future edition.

This guidebook aims to include all of the critical details necessary for an enjoyable climbing experience. For example, directions, maps, route grades, and even helpful tips and hints are included. Notice, however, that first-ascent or route-originator information isn't included. Though this information is a critical piece of Oregon's climbing history, it isn't absolutely necessary for someone to find and climb a route. Plus, credible climbing histories are difficult to obtain for a majority of backcountry areas.

SAFETY

Before venturing off into the bounty of climbing Oregon has to offer, understand that all safety rules apply. Some areas in this book are considered "backcountry" climbing areas because a designated owner or caretaker does not maintain them. Climbing in many of these areas can be more dangerous than climbing in a state park, city, or town, and emergency assistance is not as readily available. Many of these routes are older than

Adam making a clip on *Right on Joe* (5.10a) at Meadow Picnic Area.

your typical sport routes in a well-developed park. In turn, the difficulty grading is different. For example, a backcountry 5.7 could grade at 5.8 or 5.9- by Smith Rock standards. Routes with extreme grading discrepancies have been adjusted to be more in line with today's standards. Also, bolts are typically spaced farther apart on backcountry routes. Fixed protection is not checked as regularly as in parks, and loose rock is not removed as often either. Climb with an experienced climber if you are a beginner or new to the area.

ETHICS

Last but not least, remember your ethics and responsibilities as a climber. In some states and regions, climbing areas are being closed down faster than they are being developed. We don't want Oregon's climbing areas to end up in the same situation. Climb ethically by limiting fixed protection whenever possible, using chalk sparingly, and always cleaning up your mess. Develop routes ethically, too. Limit pruning and cleaning as much as possible while still creating safe routes for everyone to enjoy. Before bolting, ask around and know the area's history. Special regulations and limits apply to a lot of areas. Finally, obey access signs and respect property rights. Several climbing areas are accessible solely because of a landowner's graciousness. A little respect and a little care can go a long way in maintaining good climber-landowner relations.

We hope this information provides you with many safe, fun climbing adventures. Enjoy!

HOW TO USE THIS BOOK

SAMPLE AREA DESCRIPTION TABLE

Rock Type	Limestone
Quality of Rock (0–5)	5
Maximum Height	65 feet
Ownership	BLM

This sample description table summarizes some information about the climbing area. Most of it is self-explanatory, but the following guidelines have been used to determine a subjective grade for **rock quality.**

A **5** rating denotes impeccable rock. This rock is solid and clean and protects well. It is nearly perfect, with no moss, no loose sections, and no dirt or debris. Smith Rocks and Yosemite Valley rock are representative of quality 5.

A **4** rating means the rock is very solid and clean. It is excellent rock for climbing, and the smallest holds can be trusted not to break. Rock rated 4 is every bit as good as 5, but very small portions may have minimal moss or debris. Rock rated 5 also may be downgraded to 4 if the rock is sharper than normal or slick in sections. Volcanic columns such as those found on Devils Tower are representative of quality 4 rock.

A **3** rating should be considered average rock quality for most climbing areas. The rock is solid and trustworthy, but may be mossy or slightly dirty in sections. This rock may be more difficult to protect with traditional gear. It may possess qualities such as being slippery in sections, or grainy, or having small amounts of loose rock present. Zion National Park sandstone and Joshua Tree granite are representative of the 3 rating, given their grainy and/or slippery nature.

A **2** rating is mostly solid but should not be considered entirely trustworthy without first checking. This rock will have some loose sections, debris, or excessive moss. Small holds may not be solid and should be considered suspect. Rock rated 2 may also be excessively sharp or slippery by nature. It may be difficult to make solid placements on this rock with traditional gear. The sand-covered sandstone of Patrick's Point State Park in California is representative of quality 2 rock.

Rock rated **1** significantly lessens the climbing experience given its suspect nature. It should be considered loose or dirty. It is rarely solid enough to protect with traditional gear and should only be toproped. Rock rated 1 may be excessively sharp or slippery and will contain lots of loose debris. Extreme caution should be taken when climbing on this rock. An area representative of such poor rock quality would include the uncleaned portions of Smith Rock's upper pinnacles.

Rock rated **0** should be totally avoided given its suspect nature and its impacts on climber safety. It is likely loose and offers poor protection.

Note that aggressive cleaning can turn quality 2 rock into quality 4 or 5 with the removal of dirt, moss, other debris, and loose rock. While aggressive cleaning is not encouraged, the removal of dangerous debris and loose rock in a safe manner may be

RATING SYSTEM COMPARISON CHART

YDS	British	French	Australian	UIAA
5.3	VD 3b	2	11	II
5.4	HVD 3c	3	12	III
5.5	MS/S/HS 4a	4a	12/13	IV
5.6	HS/S 4a	4b	13	V-
5.7	HS/VS 4b/4c	4c	14/15	V/V+
5.8	HVS 4c/5a	5a	16	V+
5.9	HVS 5a	5b	17	VI
5.10a	E1 5a/5b	5c	18	VI+
5.10b	E1/E2 5b/5c	6a	19	VI+
5.10c	E2/E3 5b/5c	6a+	20	VII-
5.10d	E3 5c/6a	6b	21	VII
5.11a	E3/E4 5c/6a	6b+	22	VII+
5.11b	E4/E5 6a/6b	6c	22/23	VII+
5.11c	E4/E5 6a/6b	6c+	23	VIII-
5.11d	E4/E5 6a/6b	7a	24	VIII
5.12a	E5 6b/6c	7a+	25	VIII+
5.12b	E5/E6 6b/6c	7b	26	VIII+/IX-
5.12c	E5/E6 6b/6c/7a	7b+	27	IX-
5.12d	E6/E7 6c/7a	7c	28	IX
5.13a	E6/E7 6c/7a	7c+	28/29	IX+
5.13b	E7 7a	8a	29	X-
5.13c	E7 7a	8a+	30	X-/X
5.13d	E8 7a	8b	31	X
5.14a	E8 7a	8b+	32	X+
5.14b	E9 7a	8c	33	XI-
5.14c	E9 7b	8c+	34	XI
5.14d	E10 7b	9a	35	XI+

acceptable if it improves the safety and climbing experience for subsequent climbers. Rock should only be cleaned with the consideration of environmental, biological, and aesthetic impacts.

SAMPLE ROUTE DESCRIPTION

5. Jesus Saves (5.11a) ★★★ This is a difficult, right-facing arête.

Each description starts with the **route number.** Routes are renumbered beginning with 1 at the start of each climbing area. Corresponding numbers are used on the topos.

Next comes the **route name.** Many original route names, part of the public domain, were gathered through prepublished information and secondary data sources. Original route names could not be collected for some routes. In this case, nicknames not created by route originators or setters are used. The intent is to create a common name to be used in conversation and for reference. Updates and corrections are welcome and appreciated.

Next is the **difficulty rating.** Route difficulty ratings are described using the Yosemite Decimal System (YDS). The YDS contains two unique difficulty identifiers and ranges from 1 to 5.15a. The first number, 1 through 5, depicts the general difficulty of a route. One is the easiest; this would typically be a hike on flat ground. Five is the most difficult; these routes are considered technical climbs. Class 5 routes contain a second number that comes after the period, 1 through 15a. This depicts the difficulty of the technical route. One is the easiest; the most difficult is 15a. Grades 10 through 15 are further broken down and are typically followed by a letter, a (the easiest) through d (the most difficult).

Some original route difficulty grades, facts of the public domain, were gathered through prepublished information and secondary data sources. Original difficulty grades could not be obtained for some routes. For consistency, the authors have included primary data for about 75 percent of the routes in this guidebook. These routes were climbed personally or by a regular climbing partner. Grades should be accurate within plus or minus one number, but as always, you are responsible for choosing routes within your abilities, regardless of the grade they are assigned.

Most topos do not include bolts. Because many of the routes in this book are one pitch, it is usually possible to count the bolts while standing at the base of the cliff. Always bring along a couple of spare quickdraws just in case. As for anchors, unless otherwise noted, they will be found at the top of the route line on the topo.

Finally, we have included a **route quality grade.** This is a subjective scale ranging from zero to three stars (★). This scale takes into account the rock quality, length of the route, and type of moves required to complete the route. Zero stars indicates a low-quality route. Three stars depict an excellent route, one that is highly recommended.

Map Legend

Borders

State Border	— - — - —
State Park	//////////

Transportation

Interstate	84
US/State Highway	26
Paved Road	58
Gravel Road	======
Unimproved Road	= = = = = =
Established Trail	----------
Informal Trail	----------

Hydrology

Lake	
Stream	
River / Creek	
Intermittent	

Physiography

Cliff / Scarp	
Peak	▲
Boulder	●

Symbols

Bridge	
Campground	⛺
Climbing Area	■
Dam	＼
Golf Course	
Parking	P
Point of Interest	■
Rappel Station	o→
Trailhead	·
Visitor Center	?

Population

Capital	✪
City	◉
Town	○

EASTERN OREGON

BURNT RIVER CANYON

Rock Type	Limestone
Quality of Rock (0–5)	5
Maximum Height	65 feet
Ownership	BLM

■ OVERVIEW

Burnt River Canyon is a steep, narrow
canyon lined with dirt hills and rock buttresses. This area hosts several high-quality
sport climbs, with the level of climbing ranging from beginner to expert. There are plenty
of difficult routes for expert climbers; nearly
40 percent of the routes grade 5.11 and
harder. It takes several days to climb all of the
routes in a particular grade. The rock is well
developed, but there's a lot more room for
new routes. All routes are bolted, and the
bolts are solid and well spaced. There are no
permanent trails, but most rocks are close to
the road, so trails are not necessary. Climbing
year-round is possible. Summer months can

be quite hot, while winter temperatures can
be very low. Few areas are shaded from the
sun. The rock is clean and solid. Divots,
pockets, edges, and flakes all make good
holds. Ticks and rattlesnakes are common.
The area is very arid, and the canyon walls
often block visibility to approaching weather,
so be prepared and take the necessary precautions. The canyon is abundant with free
camping areas, but drinking water and restrooms are unavailable. The nearest services
are located in Baker City, 33 miles north.

Finding the cliffs: From Baker City, follow
Interstate 84 southeast. Go 22 miles to the
town of Durkee, and take exit 327. Drive to
the stop sign at the junction of Vandecar
Road. Turn west onto Vandecar Road, toward
the town of Durkee, and drive 0.5 mile
through town. Turn northwest (right) onto
Old Highway 30 at the stop sign after the
railroad tracks. Follow Old Highway 30 for
1.5 miles and turn west (left) onto Burnt
River Canyon Lane. Drive 11 miles to the
first climbing area. This gravel road is narrow
and has steep banks, and traffic is common.
Drive cautiously.

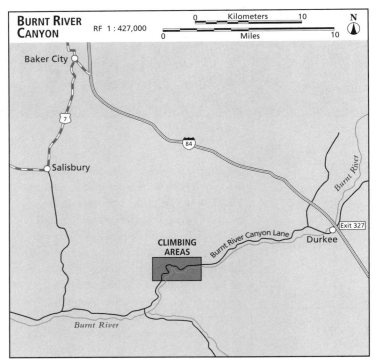

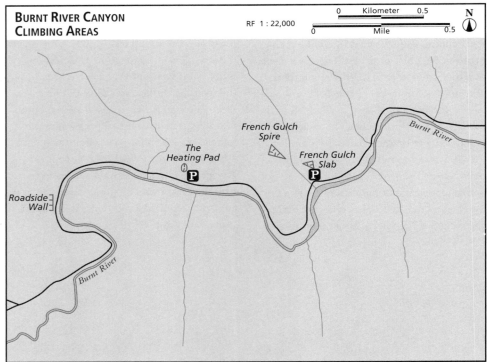

Burnt River Canyon is a steep, narrow canyon lined with dirt hills and rock buttresses.

French Gulch Spire

French Gulch Slab

French Gulch

French Gulch Slab

French Gulch Slab, the first good limestone buttress as approached from the east, is a common first stop. The routes are good to warm up on. The rock is about 45 feet tall and lies 15 feet off the road. Park on the short road paralleling the small creek that flows into the Burnt River. Little Gray Buttress is located on the small creek's east side.

1. Felcos Demise (5.8) ★★★ This great route is taller than it appears. The bolts are placed well, and good holds make clipping the bolts easy. The crux comes two-thirds of the way up. A large section of blank rock separates the good holds.

2. Stranger Than Friction (5.10a) ★★ This fun route is shorter than *Felcos Demise,* though they share top anchors. The crux comes around the third bolt. The holds are smaller and are spaced out. The bolts are placed close together, which makes the route a good lead for beginners.

3. Prize Winning Fly (5.7) ★★ This short route sits the farthest right on the buttress. Climb a few feet straight up, then traverse up and left to the anchors on top of *Felcos Demise.* Most of the route is easy at 5.5. The crux requires one tricky move at the big pocket halfway up.

French Gulch Spire

French Gulch Spire is a large rock that sits on the west side of the small creek, opposite French Gulch Slab. The hike is strenuous, and no man-made trails lead to the rock, but the climbing is rewarding and well worth the hike. Start on the west side of the little creek, and hike straight for the upper section of the south wall. This approach covers steep ground; caution is required. Or, follow the main road 0.25 mile toward the Heating Pad. This approach starts on the hill's west side. Hike up the barren talus slope to the rock.

4. Corn Flakes (5.8) ★★★ This is one of the best single-pitch 5.7s in the state. Most of the route grades 5.6, but there are two 5.7 cruxes. The first lies at the very start of the route; the second comes at the third bolt. The rock and the holds are nearly perfect.

5. Raisin Bran (5.10d) ★★★ This is an excellent route. The crux spans between the third and sixth bolts. The holds are small, and the face is steep. Most climbers find stacking fingers in the small pockets to be helpful. Toward the top of the route, the holds are sloping. This section is relentless; there are few good holds on which to rest. The entire route requires precision footwork and balance. It shares top anchors with *Corn Flakes*.

6. Lime Rickey (5.7) ★★★ This section of rock is perfect. The bottom half of the route is steep, and the difficulty is sustained. Good holds keep the grade at 5.7. The crux comes at the steep section 20 feet up. Top anchors and chains are in place.

7. Chunky Dig (5.8) ★★★ This route is covered with good holds. The bottom has pockets and slits, which are interesting to climb. The crux comes at the small roof three-quarters of the way up. The rock is solid and clean. Several tricky sections require you to think before you climb.

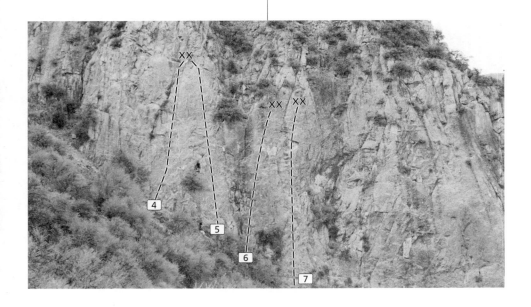

The Heating Pad

The Heating Pad is found 100 yards up the hill on the canyon's north side. It sits 100 feet west of the house with the footbridge crossing the river. Both climbs are on the rock's west side. The area provided for belaying can be very dangerous. There are no flat places to stand, and the hillside is very unstable. Bad-fall potential exists.

8. Drawing a Blank

(5.10a) ✭✭ This is a fun, short little route. The slightly overhanging crux is at the first bolt. There are few good footholds, but huge handholds make the start relatively easy. The route drops to 5.7 after the second bolt.

9. Iridescence (5.11d)

✭ The holds on this route are tiny and sharp, and climbing on them can be painful. The crux comes near the bottom. The first bolt is 20 feet off the ground. Extreme caution is advised. A clip-stick may come in handy. The rock is solid but sharp through the crux. The grade drops after the second bolt.

Routes

Roadside Wall Overview

The Roadside Wall

This is a neat area. The Roadside Wall is only 150 feet up the hill from the road, located on the north side of the river. The climbs are about 45 feet tall, and most of them are overhanging. All of the climbs are relatively difficult, but they are also very enjoyable. The wall sits behind some trees, which provide shade for hot days. There are not any good parking areas available. Pull off the road as much as possible.

10. Slab (5.10c) ★★ The bottom of this route is steep. Many climbers' arms are spent by the time they reach the technical crux, which comes at the fifth bolt. This section requires a long reach from the outside corner to a sloping ledge on the right with no good footholds. The bottom is clean, but the top 15 feet is mossy and slick.

11. Dog Gone (5.11b) ★★ The sustained crux spans the bottom 25 feet of the route. This series of moves is very strenuous. The start is aggressively overhanging, and the top gets difficult as well. The rock is flat and somewhat mossy. The good holds are spaced far apart.

12. Time Warp (5.11d) ★★★ The bottom 15 feet is overhanging but has good holds. Climb up and right to the bottom of the bulge. Several great holds lie to the right of the bolts. These holds are critical in getting past the bulge. The bulge's top brings you to the crux of the route, which comes at the last bolt. Be aware of the slopers through this balancy section.

13. If Clips Could Kill (5.11a) ★★★ This route climbs perfect rock and is very steep and pumpy. The crux comes between the first and second bolts, at the big overhang. The very top is tricky. Most climbers are tired at this point, and the good holds are hidden and must be searched out.

ANTHONY LAKE

Rock Type	Granite
Quality of Rock (0–5)	4
Maximum Height	450 feet
Ownership	USFS

■ OVERVIEW

Anthony Lake provides the only reasonable access to Oregon's granite. The area provides one-pitch sport routes as well as multi-pitch traditional routes. The climbing level ranges from beginner to intermediate, with routes ranging from 5.4 to 5.10a. The granite is mostly solid with moss and lichen covering some portions of the uncleaned rock. Routes in this area provide a week or more of climbing, which is best late summer through fall. The winter brings several feet of snow, and mosquitoes thrive in the spring and early summer. This section of mountains lies between 7,000 and 9,000 feet elevation, so the climber should be prepared for any type of weather. Anthony Lake Campground has services such as drinking water and restrooms.

Finding the cliffs: From U.S. Highway 26, turn north onto Highway 7 toward Austin. Continue on Highway 7 to the junction with USFS Road 73. Turn left on USFS 73 and continue through Sumpter and Granite. Eight miles beyond Granite at the junction with USFS Road 51, continue right on USFS 73 toward the Anthony Lake Ski Area. Anthony Lake is approximately 17 miles beyond this junction.

Or, from Baker City, drive 13 miles northwest on Interstate 84 and take exit 285 to North Powder. Follow USFS 73 to Anthony Lake Ski Area. Anthony Lake is 19 miles from North Powder.

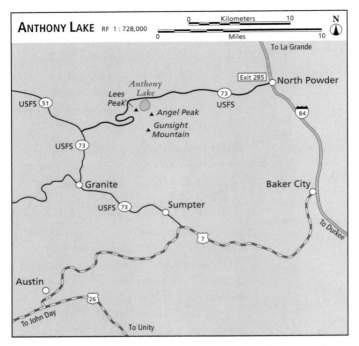

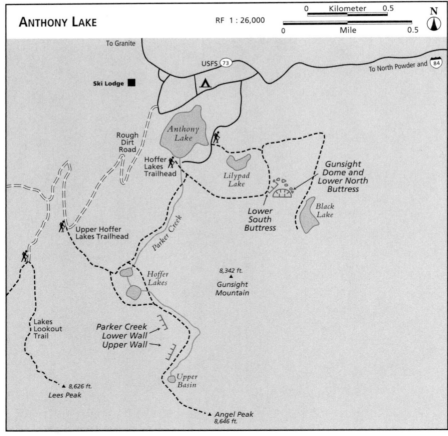

Anthony Lake provides the most accessible granite climbing in Oregon as well as some amazing scenery.

Ben searching for higher ground on the ample granite cliffs of Anthony Lake.

Gunsight Dome
North Buttress

This buttress has four climbs and is about 50 feet tall. There are no bolts on the wall, and traditional gear is needed to set up topropes. The wall is part of Gunsight Dome and lies on the bottom of the dome's north side. Green lichen on the buttress's top helps to identify it. To find the climbs, follow the hiking directions to Gunsight Dome. Continue to the north end of the talus field to the bottom of the buttress.

1. Flatman (5.7) ✷✷ This is a toprope face. Start in the crack system on the wall's east end, and climb up and over the green-lichen face. The flat crux lies two-thirds of the way up.

2. Elastic Crack (5.4) ✷ Start left of the easy, tree-covered staircase, and follow the 1- to 3-inch crack. About halfway up, trees block the crack. Climb around, up, and left, then scramble to the top. Bring long slings and anchors for setting up a top-belay.

3. Pufar's Ramp (5.5) ✷✷ This route protects well with a standard rack, except the top section. Start at the wall's base, and follow the clean crack and ramp system. Keep right of the tree-covered staircase crack. Routes 2, 3, and 4 share the same trees as top anchors.

4. Pufar's Pillagers (5.7) ✷ This is an alternate start to *Pufar's Ramp*. Start at the wall's base. Climb the easy 5.1 slab for 20 feet to a nearly vertical 5.7 crack in the left wall, then climb the crack for 15 feet. The route then joins *Pufar's Ramp* to the finish.

Gunsight Dome Lower South Buttress

There are no bolts or top anchors in place on this buttress. Long slings and traditional gear are required for setting up topropes. The buttress is about 35 feet tall. To reach it, start at the Hoffer Lakes Trailhead next to the boat dock parking area, and follow the trail for 50 feet. Turn left and follow the trail around the south side of Lilypad Meadow. Continue along the trail to the northeast side of the meadow. Directly below Gunsight Dome's southwest side, follow a faint trail up the hill and hike 100 yards to the Lower South Buttress. Several small trails run through the area. Many climbers have a difficult time finding the buttress.

5. Dr. Evil's Crack (5.7) ✶
Start at the parallel cracks on the pillar's right (south) side. The cracks can be slightly difficult to protect with gear. Climb the cracks, then traverse up the arête to the summit.

6. Mojo Moves (5.7) ✶✶ This route protects well enough with traditional gear to be led. The crux comes at the bottom's steep section. The rock and moves are enjoyable.

7. Scott's Staircase (5.4) ✶✶ This line makes an easy toprope. It is commonly free-soloed. Climb the staircase crack, then diagonal up and left to the top.

8. Flatbastard (5.5) ✶✶ This is a fun, easy ramp. Climb straight up the west face of the buttress. Traditional gear is necessary to set up a toprope.

Gunsight Dome

Gunsight Dome is a large dome-shaped peak that lies on a ridge about 0.5 mile north of Gunsight Mountain. This dome's face is a steep ramp capped by a small ceiling. Many variations exist; some are more runout than others. There are no bolts on the dome, and traditional gear is needed. To reach the dome, hike to Gunsight Dome Lower South Buttress, and proceed directly up the hill another 150 yards. A talus field lies at the dome's bottom. Hike north on the edge of the talus and the timber. *Zig Zag a Roof*'s start is found two-thirds of the way to the dome's north side. Belay below the most solid line of rock coming down the ramp. Several large, flat boulders make a convenient staging area.

To descend, hike down the northwest ridge to the Black Lake Trail, then follow a maze of connecting trails back to the dome's bottom. Or, rappel off a low set of trees on the dome's south side. From the correct tree, a single 60-meter rope lowers you far enough to scramble back to the route's bottom. Rappelling down is recommended versus taking Black Lake Trail.

9. Zig Zag a Roof (5.7) ★★★ This three-pitch route winds its way up the face's prominent crack system. It is a great climb. The middle pitch can be runout, and the crack is full of debris. Leading is not recommended for timid climbers. This route can be climbed in two pitches, but three pitches is strongly recommended to reduce rope drag. **Pitch 1:** (5.7) Start below the solid line of rock on the dome's left side. Scramble up several ramps to a vertical 15-foot-tall wall. Use good holds to climb straight up the wall's 5.7 middle. Belay on a ledge on the wall's top. **Pitch 2:** (5.5) Move up and right 20 feet to the large diagonal crack splitting the dome's face. Follow the crack up and right for 35 feet to an old, rusty piton. Change direction and follow the intersecting crack, up and left for 20 feet. Belay 15 feet below the ceiling. Use long runners to reduce rope drag. **Pitch 3:** (5.7) Climb straight up to the overhanging ceiling. Use finger jams to traverse the 5.7 section to a corner. Climb steep rock for 6 feet to gain the ceiling's top. Scramble up 20 feet, and belay off a large tree.

Rappel
Tree

9

Lower Parker Creek Wall

A low-angle wall runs the distance of Parker Creek. There are two climbable sections, called the upper and lower walls. To reach the lower wall, hike 100 yards up Parker Creek from South Hoffer Lakes, toward the Upper Basin. Look closely for bolts to identify the climbing area.

10. Cammin' Away

(5.7) ★★ This easy traditional route makes a nice warm-up. Extra gear and slings are needed to set up a top-belay. The route protects well with a standard rack. The top requires 4-inch gear. Some portions of the crack are dirty.

Brian starting up *Cammin' Away.*

11. Angled Assassin (5.9) ★★★ This is a fun sport climb. The overhanging start is tricky; use the great holds to pull over it. The balancy crux comes on tiny edges above the third bolt. Top anchors are not in place. Use traditional gear and longs slings to set up a top-belay.

12. Sticky Nails (5.10a) ★★★ This is another classic sport climb. It is well protected. The superflat crux at the third bolt is made possible by the route's angle. Top anchors are in place.

Upper Parker Creek Wall

To reach the wall, start at the upper Hoffer Lakes Trailhead, which is halfway up the four-wheel-drive road to the Lakes Lookout. Follow the trail to Hoffer Lakes, then hike up Parker Creek for 300 yards. The wall is obviously larger and cleaner than the rest of the rock. It lies only 200 feet down the creek from the Upper Basin.

13. North Flake (5.6) ★★ Climb the solid flake to the wall's top. The crux comes near the top while using the crack to exit the small ceiling. The route protects fairly well. There are two bolts on top for a belay.

14. Sweet Thing (5.8 R) ★★★ Two bolts are on top for a belay. The crux comes at the route's start. The crack is very shallow and difficult to protect. The rock is clean, and the moves are fluid. This is one of the best routes at Anthony Lake.

15. Chisel Queen (5.9) ★★ This face makes a great toprope. Use tiny edges to climb the blank face between the two cracks. The top gets easier. Belay off *Sweet Thing's* top anchors.

16. Wide Bottom (5.5) ★ Large protection is needed

to protect this crack system. Climb straight up the wide crack. Stem and balance off the surrounding features. There is only one bolt on top for a belay. Use traditional protection or the anchors on top of *Sweet Thing* to supplement the top belay.

Angel Peak and Lees Peak

Lees Peak

Lees Peak's north-face ramp is a great climb. The protection can be sparse, and there are no bolts on the mountain. To reach the route, drive the road to the Lakes Lookout Trailhead, and hike toward the Lakes Lookout. About halfway to the mountain, descend the ridge on the left. There are multiple gullies here; use a shallow one without loose rock. Scramble over the talus field to the ramp's bottom. Descend by taking the Lakes Lookout Trail back to the trailhead.

17. Runaway Ramp (5.6 R) ★★★ This climb is a classic. The final pitch is not necessary. Use long runners to reduce rope drag. **Pitch 1:** (5.5) Start on the ramp's

*See separate topo for Pitch 4

right side. Use a 10-inch cam to protect the bottom 30 feet. Climb 65 feet and belay on a small ledge. **Pitch 2:** (5.4) Climb 60 feet straight up the ramp, staying just left of the ramp's middle. Belay in the 3-foot-deep gully in the ramp's middle, 20 feet below some small trees. **Pitch 3:** (5.4) Climb 40 feet to a dirt bench on the ramp's left side. Climb another 10 feet of rock to a dirt ramp and make a belay, or continue across the dirt ramp and belay below the fourth pitch.

Pitch 4: (5.6) Above the dirt gully, a nice face and crack system leads to the top of the mountain's west summit. Jam the crack and climb the big ledges to the summit. Belay on top. Rappel down, or downclimb 15 feet to the trail. This is one of the finest hand-jam cracks at Anthony Lake.

17 (Pitch 4)

Start to Avoid Snow

Original start

18

Descent Trail

Angel Peak

Angel Peak's northwest face is about 450 feet tall. There are no bolts or fixed protection on the mountain. Traditional gear is needed for all climbing. To reach the route, start at the upper Hoffer Lakes Trailhead, which lies halfway up the rough dirt road to the Lakes Lookout. Follow the trail to Hoffer Lakes, then follow Parker Creek to the Upper Basin. Continue toward the saddle between the two mountains. When appropriate, turn left and hike 200 yards to Angel Peak's base.

18. Free Ride to Heaven (5.6) ✭✭✭ This is a classic, multi-pitch rock climb. The approach's scenery is beautiful. The protection is runout in some sections, but these sections are easy and the rock is very solid. The ramp is sheltered from the sun, and the upper portion can hold snow into late summer. Extreme caution must be used when climbing below snowpacks. **Pitch 1:** (5.3)

Start below the prominent crack system on the ramp's right side, and climb straight up the cracks for 70 feet. Belay in a shallow groove with a large crack exiting the top. If snow blocks the route, start left under the crescent-shaped roof. Traverse up and right until joining the regular route. **Pitch 2:** (5.5) Climb up the crack system for 150 feet to a shallow ledge. Belay from the ledge, which lies halfway between the first pitch's crescent-shaped roof and the large grassy ledge above. **Pitch 3:** (5.6) Climb up 50 feet, then diagonal up and left 70 feet to a large grassy ledge. Belay on this ledge, or continue another 30 feet and belay on the upper, smaller grassy ledge. A portion of the upper ledge is covered by snow nearly year-round. **Pitch 4:** (5.6) Move up and right for 60 feet to the saddle between Angel Peak's upper and lower summits. A belay can be set up using the big boulders at the ramp's top. This pitch can be tricky to protect. Several pockets in the rock

18 Snow Start

18 Original Start

protect well with cams. **Pitch 5:** (5.1) Scramble up a shallow chimney for 30 feet to the lower west-peak summit. This pitch is commonly done without ropes or protection. **Descent:** Start between the two pinnacles on the lower west-peak summit. Hike west following a faint trail below the north-west ridge. The trail leads down and left. A few easy 6- to 10-foot downclimbs are required. Follow the faint trail for 400 yards to the saddle between Angel and Lees Peaks. Hike down the saddle back to Parker Creek and the Hoffer Lakes Trail.

HIGH VALLEY

Rock Type	Andesite
Quality of Rock (0–5)	4
Maximum Height	50 feet
Ownership	Private

■ O V E R V I E W

The High Valley climbing area comprises three separate climbing crags, all within a half mile of each other. It lies in an arid valley at the foothills of the Wallowa Mountains. The area hosts a number of high-quality sport and traditional routes. The difficulty of climbing makes the area well suited for beginner- and expert-level climbers. Route grades range from 5.4 to 5.12a. It is well developed, with good trails and top anchors in place on all climbs. The rock is hard and blocky andesite, making for superb acrobatic climbing. Routes in this area provide a week or more of climbing. Climbing is best spring through fall, but is also accessible during the winter. Traditional gear is needed for some routes, and a few require long runners on top-belays to limit rope drag.

The climate is arid. Rattlesnakes exist and bees are abundant, so take the necessary precautions. This is private property in which the landowner is allowing access for climbing. Climbers are solely responsible for their own safety and belongings. As always, in no way is the landowner responsible for actions or events that may occur from the use of this land. Obey access signs, don't make new trails, be polite, and keep the area clean. Pay camping is available east of Cove, where services such as water and restrooms are available. Free camping is available on Boise tree-farm property several miles northeast on Bates Lane.

Finding the cliffs: From La Grande, take Interstate 84 south to exit 265. Exit onto Highway 203 and follow it southeast for 10 miles to the town of Union. Upon entering Union, turn left (east) onto Highway 237 toward the town of Cove and continue for 0.1 mile. At the 90-degree left turn, continue straight onto High Valley Road and follow it for 3.5 miles until it turns to gravel.

The first cliff with a bolted route, Entrance Park, lies on the road's south side 0.4 mile from the start of the gravel. The parking area and Parking Lot Rock are 0.5 mile from the start of the gravel on the road's south side. The Main Wall lies 150 yards uphill from the parking area on the road's north side.

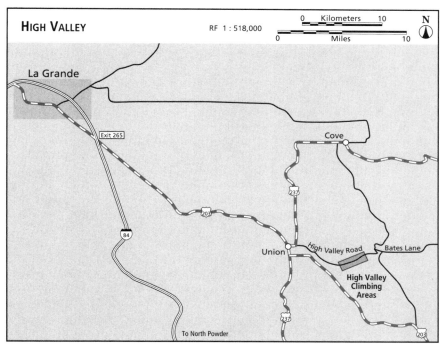

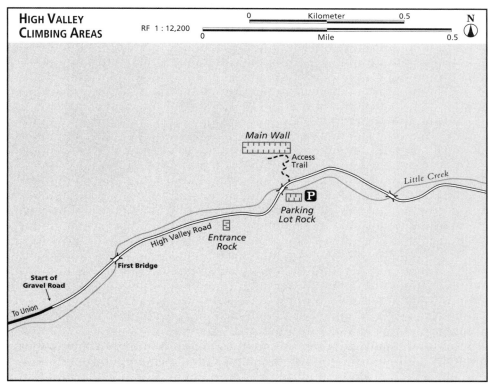

The High Valley climbing area comprises three climbing crags in the foothills of the Wallowa Mountains.

Entrance Rock

Entrance Rock contains one sport route of medium grade. The rock lies approximately 3 feet from the road. Consequently, its bottom can become dusty during dry periods. The rock lies 0.4 mile from the start of the gravel.

1. Subject to Change (5.10a) ✶✶ This dreadful-looking line sends fair rock and is actually a fun climb. The bolt spacings are nice and close. Start on the rock's right side next to the road. The route's overhanging top portion is a test of endurance. The technical crux comes at the second bolt.

Parking Lot Rock

This unique wall lies directly above a creek. A built-up belay area makes this a very comfortable climbing wall. The rock is next to the main parking area. Parking is available on either side of the road. The rock lies one half-mile from the start of the gravel. The *Parking Overhang* route makes this worth the stop. The cool creek and morning shade make for a pleasant climbing area in the hot summer.

2. Parking Overhang (5.11b) ★★★ This sport route sends the large overhang on the block's right side. It is short but powerful. Start right of the first bolt, then move up and left to the blank face and arête. Tackle the huge overhang on good holds through the powerful crux to the top-chains.

3. Steve's Wonder (5.11a) ★★ This is the first sport route put up at High Valley. The steep overhanging crux comes at the route's start. Send a series of long lock-offs on good holds. Continue up the arête and steep face to the top-chains.

4. Master Blaster (5.10a) ★ This gently overhanging line is plagued with dusty-slick rock. Climb past three bolts, then move right and join *Steve's Wonder* to the top-chains. The crux comes between the third and fourth bolts.

5. Unknown (5.10a) ★ This short, old route has had its hangers removed. It can be aided using wires over the bolts and then toproped. There are many other better routes in the area.

Main Wall

The Main Wall hosts several nice sport and traditional routes and has the greatest concentration of good routes at High Valley. Park in the main parking area next to Parking Lot Rock. The trail starts on the road's north side, just east of the small bridge. Follow the obvious trail past several switchbacks for 150 yards to the Main Wall.

6. Long Reach (5.11a) ★★★ This sport route is the farthest-right bolted line on the Main Wall. The bolts are closely spaced. Scramble past one bolt to a large overhanging face. The obvious crux comes at the third bolt. The overhang is intimidating, but the holds are very solid. Dyno to the camper above the third bolt, then power through to the top-chains.

7. Unfinished Project (5.10b) A few feet left of *Long Reach* lies an unfinished line with bolts but no hangers.

8. Chimney Face (5.10d) ★★★ Follow several bolts on great rock up the gently overhanging face. The balancy crux comes between the second and third bolts. This sustained line does not let up much after the difficult crux.

9. God's Valley Chimney (5.4) ★ This traditional route is set back between two prominent faces. There are no top anchors in place. Climb jumbled rock following two parallel cracks, then squeeze through the chimney at the route's top. One can walk off the east side of the Main Wall.

10. Fret Arête (5.9) ★★★ This excellent sport route is an area classic. It sends perfect rock. Climb the fun face to the overhanging

arête. Slap and heel hook the arête, stretching through great holds, and power through to the top-chains. Bring a ½- to ¾-inch cam to protect the runout between the first and second bolts. The crux comes at the third bolt.

11. Insomnia (5.6) ✹✹ This traditional route climbs the crack splitting the block's face. It protects well with large gear. Climb the crack and stem the outside faces up the sustained rock.

12. Elvis is Everywhere (5.12a) ✹✹✹ This gently ramped face looks easy, but don't let the looks fool you. Send the powerful and bouldery start to the first bolt, then balance on tiny fingery holds the rest of the way to the top-chains. The puzzling crux comes between the route's third and fourth bolts.

13. Classic Crack (5.8) ✹✹ This traditional route sends the dihedral created by the two faces. The wide crack requires large gear toward its top. Stemming the blank right-side face tests one's endurance. It shares top-chains with *Elvis is Everywhere.*

14. Trish's Dilemma (5.6) ✹✹✹ Climb the large and positive holds up the broken face. This is a fun traditional climb and protects well. Climb the crack system on the face's right side to the top-bolts. The steep crux comes halfway up the route. The top-bolts do not have chains, making rappelling impractical. The route must be cleaned and then walked off.

15. Thanks Keith (5.10a) ★★★ One can start on the block's right or left side. Climb large holds 20 feet to the block's top and the first bolt. The route sends the right side of the prominent face above. Use the arête and face to climb past several bolts to a prominent ceiling. The crux comes at the ceiling. Move up and to the ceiling's left side. Step up, then climb the arête and large holds to the top-chains.

16. Spacey Face (5.8) ★★★ This area classic is one of the tallest and best routes at High Valley. Start at the bottom of the face on its left side, and climb the spine to the ramp-face above. Continue on balancy but good holds to the top-bolts. The top-bolts are set back at least 10 feet from the cliff's edge. Bring long runners to reduce rope drag, or use *Thanks Keith*'s top-chains. The crux comes at the steep section between the fourth and fifth bolts.

17. Dusty Devil (5.8) ★ Jam and stem the steep crack and blank faces to the cliff's top. The route protects well with large traditional gear. A large plant in the upper part of the crack makes this route fairly unpleasant.

18. La Siesta Tick Attack (5.11b R) ★★ The route's bottom 25 feet is unprotected. Climb the steep flat face for 25 feet to the first bolt, then step left to a large ledge. Climb tiny and balancy holds up the left-side face to another bolt. Continue another 20 feet of runout to the bolts on the cliff's top.

19. Wasp Roast (5.10d) ★★★ Follow the right side of the bolt line to the second bolt. At the second bolt, traverse up and left through the crux to the better holds on the

face's left side. Climb good holds on steep rock to the final bulge. Stay to the bulge's left side, then step up and right onto the face. Pull up and over the face to the top-chains.

20. Do or Fly (5.10c) ✹✹✹ This traditional route sends the crack splitting the large blocks. A lower, 10- crux comes as one steps off the block onto the ramp-face. Jam and smear the smooth crack for 25 feet to the large overhang. Jam the crack and stem the smooth overhanging faces through the powerful crux to the top-chains. It shares top anchors with *AMPD*.

21. AMPD (5.11a) ✹✹✹ This bolted line sends a smooth ramp, then tackles the large overhang above. A lower, 10- crux comes as one steps off the block onto the ramp-face and the first bolt. Climb the sustained technical face past several bolts to the large overhang. Crimp a small ledge, then dyno to a huge hold on the face's left side. Make several strenuous moves through the steep overhang to the top-chains.

SPRING MOUNTAIN

Rock Type	Andesite
Quality of Rock (0–5)	5
Maximum Height	110 feet
Ownership	USFS

■ OVERVIEW

Spring Mountain hosts a multitude of sport and traditional routes. The level of climbing ranges from beginner to expert, with several routes grading above 5.11. It takes several weeks to climb all the routes in one's grade. The area is well developed, with good trails and a sectioned-off parking area. The cliff band lies above 4,000 feet. The climbing season starts in summer and runs through fall; snow blocks access during winter and spring. At this altitude the weather can change quickly, and rattlesnakes and yellow jackets can be a nuisance. Take the necessary precautions. Trees and open sections create shaded and sunny climbing. The rock's quality is excellent. Like basalt, it offers smooth cracks, pockets, edges, slopers, and sticky faces. The variety of holds makes this a great training area. Many of the first bolts are set up high; a clip-stick is recommended. Projects are tagged with red markers. Please respect the route setters and do not climb these routes. The local route setters have done a great job developing the area. Free camping is available throughout the area, but drinking water and restrooms are not.

Finding the crags: Drive west from La Grande on Interstate 84 for 17 miles. Take exit 243 to Summit Road and Mount Emily. Turn north onto Summit Road toward the Whitman Route Overlook, and follow this gravel road for a little less than 9 miles. Turn left on USFS Road 3109 toward the Whitman Route Overlook. Drive about 0.7 mile and turn right on the first good, gravel road, then continue 0.25 mile to the parking area. The trail starts on the north side of several small boulders at the road's end. Follow an overgrown road north for 60 feet, then turn left and follow the trail up the hill and through a clear-cut. The rock is 0.25 mile up the hill.

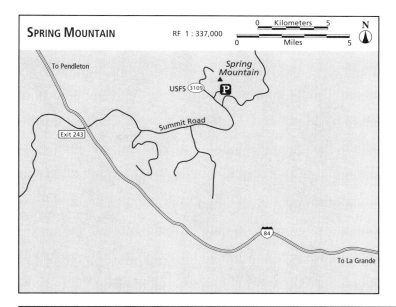

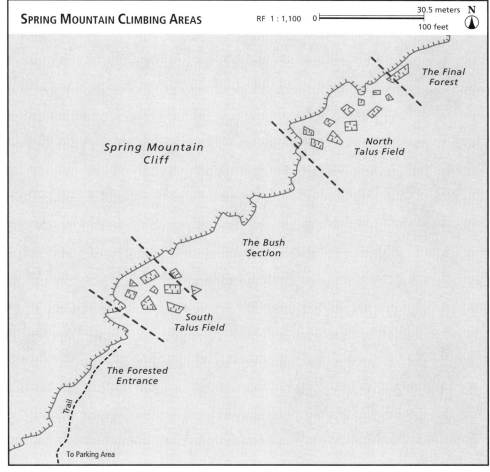

Spring Mountain provides a plethora of sport and traditional routes with excellent rock quality.

The Forested Entrance

This is the first section encountered from the trail. An abundance of trees provide shaded climbing. This section of the cliff is shorter than the rest.

1. Gome Boy (5.11a) ★ Not pictured. This is the cliff's first sport route. The route's start is tricky; the first bolt lies high up. Sloping ledges finish the route.

2. Beginner's Route (5.4) ★★ Not pictured. This little ramp lies around the corner from *Gome Boy* and can be toproped by hiking around the cliff's south side. Solid holds and clean rock make this a good route.

3. Jack and Jill (5.10c) ★★ Not pictured. This is the next sport route after *Beginner's Route*. Climb the arête through two bolts. Traverse around to the right, and climb the steep face to the chains. The crux comes through the bottom arête.

4. A Few Tense Moments (5.10b) ★★★ Climb the crack up the small roof's left side. From there, a nice ramp leads to the top anchors. The bottom crack is great.

5. Passing Lane (5.8) ★★★ This is an excellent, long route. The first bolt is placed in an awkward position. Climb 15 feet through a small overhang, then cruise up the ramp-arête to the top.

6. Mountain Ears Route (5.6) ★★★ This good traditional route has no bolts. The crux comes at the small overhang 15 feet up. Finish by slipping through the hole under the big boulder.

7. Unnamed (5.12a) ★★★ This route covers impeccable rock. Tiny ledges lead up a steep face. The route's middle section has no good rests.

8. Welcome to Spring Mountain Left Variation (5.10c) ★★
This left-side variation tackles the big overhang off the ground. The overhanging crux has good holds. Its steepness pumps the arms.

9. Welcome to Spring Mountain (5.8) ★★
This route is dirty in spots, and its difficulty is fairly sustained. The top gets steep; use the great arête on the left to pull over it.

10. The Diving Board (5.9) ★★
The bottom pitch of this two-pitch route is good. The steep crux comes at the pitch's top. The rock is a little mossy; it is recommended to stop after the first pitch. The top is a sharp off-width crack.

11. Spider (5.11c) ★★★
This is a fun route. Start by climbing the balancy ramp. The crux comes toward the route's top. The rock is steep, and the holds are small.

12. Nurse Ratchet (5.10c) ★
This new line has yet to gain popularity, so the rock is still mossy. Climb the lower ramp, then tackle a series of small overhangs using the arête on the right. Use cams to protect the top.

13. Face the Facts (5.9) ★
The awkward crux comes before the first bolt, and the route lets up afterwards. Many holds are sloping and mossy.

14. Face the Crook (5.7) ★
The crux comes through the bottom overhang. The awkward crack makes placing protection difficult. Climb 30 feet, then step right to a shared belay with *By Hook or By Crook*.

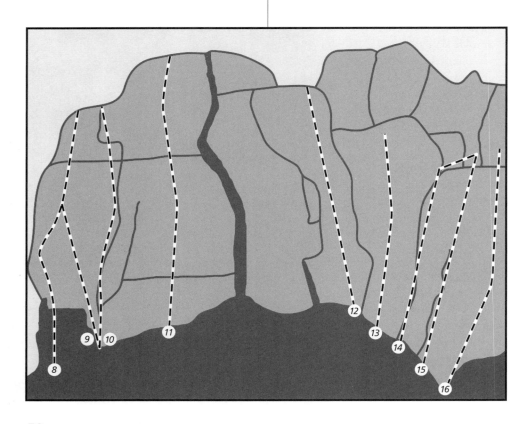

15. By Hook or By Crook (5.10d) ✶✶✶ This is a fun route. The holds are good, and its steepness pumps up the arms. The entire route is slightly overhanging.

16. Unnamed (5.11d) ✶✶✶ The bouldery crux comes at the route's start. All of the holds are decent, so it is just a power issue.

17. Exterminailer (5.7) ✶✶ Great rock and solid holds make this a good route. Some of the bolts are spaced far apart. It is recommended to step left after the fourth bolt to the set of anchors.

18. Bat Crack (5.7) ✶✶ This solid crack protects well. It is a short route. Climb the crack for 25 feet, then step right to a set of anchors.

19. Feat Petite (5.7) ✶✶ This little sport route makes a good warm-up. The crux comes at the route's top. Clipping the anchors is difficult due to a lack of good holds.

20. Captain Winkie (5.8 R) Not pictured. This route is very runout, and the holds are dirty and mossy. It is not recommended and should be avoided.

21. Skinny Hippie (5.10a) ★★★ Technical moves send this smooth face. Use the finger-crack holds. Two overhangs at the route's top test one's endurance.

22. Dog Show
(5.12a) ★★ This is a very steep, technical face. The holds are small and balancy. The top anchors are in an awkward position.

23. Eaten Alive
(5.10b) ★★ The crux comes through the route's first section. Climb the steep overhang for 20 feet. Traverse to the right, and finish up the easy ramp.

24. Clavical Crack (5.9) ★ This corner creates an awkward stemming line. The grade drops halfway up. The route joins *Eaten Alive* two-thirds of the way up.

25. Triple Threat (5.10b) ✶✶ This is a tall sport route. The technical crux comes at the first bolt. The top block is steep, flat, and tiring. There are three blocks to climb. Climb the ramp for 30 feet. Traverse right and climb the 25-foot-tall overhanging block. Continue up the steep block another 30 feet to the top anchors, which lie just below the cliff's top.

26. Cruisin' for a Bruisin' (5.9) ✶✶ This nice crack protects well. The lieback crux comes at the route's top.

27. Crimp or Wimp (5.11a) ✶✶✶ Perfect rock makes this a great route. It is a one-hit wonder, and most of the route is easy. The difficult crux lies below the third bolt. The route gets thin, balancy, and overhanging.

28. Flaked Out (5.9) ★★★ This route's edgy start is unique. The crux comes at its top. Traverse the flake to the exposed face, then step up to the anchors.

29. Sphincks Crack (5.9) ★★ This jumbled crack is set in an open book. The crack's shape makes protection tricky. The awkward crux comes at the bulge, 20 feet up.

30. Mojo Rising (5.11a) ★★★ This is a superfun, long, overhanging face. There are lots of great holds, and its steepness pumps the arms. Use the nice resting ledge halfway up.

31. Aloha Direct (5.8) ★★ This fun, little, steep face makes a good route. The crux comes at the second bolt. Climb up for 30 feet, then step right and join routes with *Hawaiian Slab.*

32. Hawaiian Slab (5.5) ★★★ This is one of the best 5.5s in all of Oregon's backcountry. Its clean ramp makes a great beginner lead-climb. The crux comes between the second and third bolts.

33. Split Decision (5.10d) ★★ Start at the belay on *Hawaiian Slab*'s top. Climb the smooth, flat face for 30 feet to another set of anchors.

34. Funny Trumpets Arête (5.9 R) This is a runout ramp, with older bolts and a poor belay area. Climb the ramp's left side to the top anchors. Watch out for dirty, loose rock. This route is not recommended.

35. Noble Slabbage (5.9) ★★ This short route's bouldery crux starts with small holds. The route then lets up. The belay area is awkward.

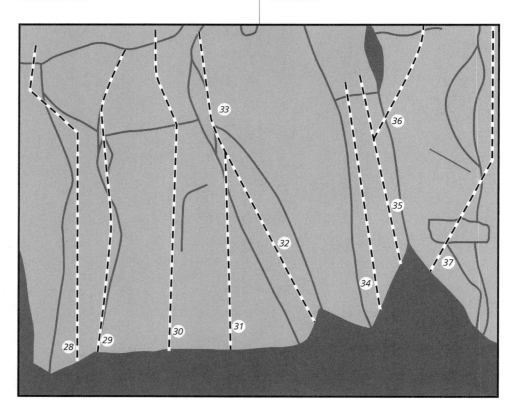

36. Shagadelick Groove (5.9) ★★ Climb the first four bolts of *Noble Slabbage*. Traverse right and cross a gully, then climb the route's top half. This is a fun, long route; it almost goes to the cliff's top. The belay area is awkward.

37. Mantle With Care (5.10d) ★★ Start at the dirty gully's top. The first bolt has no hanger; use a small nut to protect it. Climb the jumbled, steep rock to the top anchors, which lie just below the cliff's top. The crux comes at the steep bulge halfway up.

38. Breathe the Air (5.10b) ★★★ Not pictured. This is the very last route in the trees. Start at the sharp arête's bottom, and move up its left side for 45 feet to the anchors. The arête provides solid liebacks and smears for the feet. The route's difficulty is fairly sustained.

South Talus Field

This section of the cliff is not shaded. It contains many great routes.

39. Fab Slab (5.9) ★★★ This is South Talus Field's first route. Use good holds to climb through the overhang, and continue up the ramp-face to the steeper headwall. Climb the steep headwall another 25 feet to the top anchors.

40. Red (5.9) ★★★ This mixed route requires traditional gear to be protected. The crux comes at the very bottom. Climb small holds past three bolts, and follow the crack up the ramp and steeper face above. *Red* and *Fab Slab* share top anchors.

41. Triple Arthrodesis (5.5) ★★★ This great crack is set back in a nice dihedral. Work up the crack and ramp for 35 feet to the top anchors. The crack gets thin toward the top but protects well all the way.

42. Blackout (5.11b) ✭✭✭ Climb mixed holds up a steep face for 35 feet, then climb the overhanging face to the top anchors. The exciting crux comes at the overhang's top. The holds are decent, but its steepness is draining.

43. Snapped It Off

(5.10c) ✭✭✭ Climb good holds up the broken face for 30 feet. Use the right-side arête to balance up the steep face.

44. The Pod of God

(5.8) ✭✭✭ This crooked line is a great route. The top bulge can be tricky; protection can be difficult around it, and longer-fall

potential exists. The route shares anchors with *Rally Race*.

45. Rally Race (5.10b) ✭✭✭ This great route is pretty straightforward. The crux comes at the bottom. Use the flake to reach the top anchors.

46. TBA (5.11a) ★★ This mixed route has a very strenuous, overhanging start. Traditional gear is needed to protect the top crack. The route starts on the overhang's outside.

47. Initiation (5.11a) ★★★ Climb the sloped friction holds up the 40-foot ramp to the top anchors. The route covers perfect rock and has good bolt spacings.

48. Wanderer (5.6) This short, unexciting route is rarely climbed. Climb the choppy, 20-foot crack to the top anchors. Big ledges aid the ascent.

49. Blue Suede Shoes (5.7) ★★★ This is an enjoyable route that covers solid rock with good holds. Climb the angled face to a steeper, broken face and two chains.

The Bush Section

This central section of the cliff lies between the two talus fields. The bushes and few scattered trees provide little shade.

50. Epiphany (5.10b) ✮✮✮ Not pictured. This is a great route and covers perfect rock. Start 8 feet from the large ponderosa's right side, and climb 40 feet to a 4-foot ceiling. Use the great holds to power through to the top anchors.

51. Cornered (5.7) ✮✮ Not pictured. Start below the broken gray ramp and arête.

Climb the ramp for 40 feet to the top anchors. The rock is slightly dirty.

52. Get a Grip (5.11d) ✮✮✮ Not pictured. This route is very sustained, technical, and strenuous. Climb the face, traverse left, and use the arête to reach the top anchors.

53. Steppin' Out (5.11a) ✮✮ Not pictured. This route sends perfect rock. It starts a few feet right of *Get a Grip*. Use the crack through the route's middle.

54. Van Golden Brown (5.10a) ✶ This is an excellent finger and hand crack. The route's top is of poor quality. Follow the crack for 35 feet, then traverse right to *Lorraine*'s top anchors. The traverse is exposed and does not protect well.

55. On My Face (5.10c) ✶ This variation of *Van Golden Brown* makes a decent toprope. Follow *Van Golden Brown* for 20 feet, step right, and climb the thin cracks to anchors. The thin top cracks are dirty and are not climbed much.

56. Lorraine (5.10d) ✶✶✶ The steep, thin crux comes at the last bolt. This is a beautiful face and crack climb, though the lack of good rests makes it strenuous.

57. Chicken Pox (5.11a) ✶ Some of the bolts are spaced far apart; use caution clipping the second bolt. The route is very sustained with three cruxes. The rock is dirty and poor.

58. Mark's Route (5.11d) ✶✶ This route sits on the block's right side, 7 feet right of *Chicken Pox*. There are two starts, and both require a clip-stick. This difficult route sends steep rock on tiny, balancy holds.

59. Ticked (5.11a) ✶✶ This route starts in an open book. Use good holds to work through a series of bulges. The crux comes at the top bulge and requires some tricky moves.

60. Tick Spray (5.11d) ✫✫✫ This is a very sustained and strenuous route. The technical crux comes two-thirds of the way up. The bottom arête is great.

61. Frogger (5.11c) ✫ Start on the block's top, and climb the left face. Use the crack to tackle the overhanging bulge, then cruise the rounded face to the top anchors. The painful crux comes at the bulge.

62. Smackdown (5.12a) ✫✫✫ This sharp arête makes a short but excellent route. The overhanging crux comes at the arête's bottom.

63. Chunky Monkey (5.8) ✫✫ Climb the awkward, off-width crack between the face and the block. From the block's top, climb the right-side face 50 feet to the summit. Rope drag is a problem when the climb is done as one pitch. Use two ropes to rappel from the top anchors.

64. Chubby Hubby (5.12a) ✫✫✫ This is a difficult, sustained, overhanging arête. The thin, strenuous crux comes about two-thirds of the way up. It is an excellent route.

65. Freddy's Dead (5.11d) ★★ Climb through a small roof 15 feet up. Balance and toe up the pockets. Use the left-side arête. Three-quarters of the way up, move right and climb the crack and face.

66. Hang 'em Higher (5.11b) ★★ Climb the steep face moving up and left to the flat, over-hanging face. Crimp through the powerful crux.

67. Doc Holiday (5.10b) ★★ This route has brown anchors. Start on the arête's left side. On the big ledge, switch to the right. Climb the smooth ramp to the top.

68. Unnamed (5.12b) ★★ Not pictured. This route sits alone and lies 20 feet to *Doc Holiday's* right. Hike around the large gray block, then up the hill to the awk-ward belay area. Start on the easy ramp, and climb the difficult arête and face to the top anchors.

69. Arthritis (5.11b) ★★★ Not pictured. This route lies behind a small tree 20 feet right of Route 68. An excellent ½- to 1-inch crack splits a perfect face. Climb it 45 feet to the top anchors.

70. Longtime Coming (5.10a) ★★ This nice face and crack climb is fairly sustained 5.10-. Climb the crack to the top anchors. The top is slightly dirty.

71. Drama Queen (5.11d) This obvious, viscous sport climb rises up the perfect face's middle. It shares top anchors with *Hospital Corner.*

72. Hospital Corner (5.10d) ★★★ This nice crack sits in a right-facing dihedral. It protects well and offers great jams on perfect rock.

73. Puppets Without Strings (5.12a) ★★★ This is a long, difficult sport route. Lack of good rests makes them extra valuable. It offers enjoyable and fluid moves.

74. Nut Up (5.10a) ★ Climb the face and extremely thin, broken crack up the block's middle. Protection can be tricky because the crack is so thin. After 30 feet, traverse right and join *Johnny Nowhere* to the top-chains.

75. Johnny Nowhere (5.10b) ★ This dirty, old route is runout. Follow the bolts on the block's right side for 60 feet to the top-chains. The top requires traditional gear for protection. Ground-fall potential exists around the third bolt.

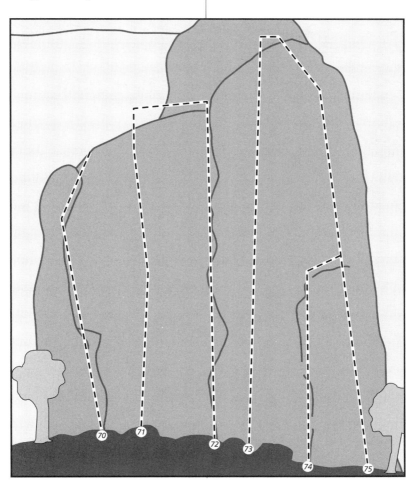

76. Summertime Arête (5.7) ★★ This route's first bolt sits high up. Start up the hill on the route's right. Traverse up and left to make the first clip, and climb the fun ramp. The exposed crux comes at the route's top. Step left and climb the good holds to the belay ledge.

77. Gidrah (5.10b) ★★ This is a two-pitch route. The first pitch is mediocre and grades 5.9. Some of the holds are mossy. The route's top has three finishes, all of which are great. The left finish grades 5.10b; the middle and right finishes grade 5.9.

78. M.T.P. (5.10c) ★★ Not pictured. This route is the next crack to the right of *Gidrah*. It lies in a nice, shallow open book. The crux comes at the huge overhang after the big hole. Continue up the bulgy, rounded face. Climb past the last four bolts of the second pitch. Use a standard rack for protection.

79. The Final Shred (5.10d) ★★★ Not pictured. This excellent face climb is identified by its colored hangers. Pitch 1 grades 5.10d. Climb the rounded face, then the arête for 50 feet to the top anchors. The bulging crux comes at the fifth bolt. The second pitch grades 5.10b. Continue up the face's left side another 45 feet to the top anchors.

80. Junior Birdman (5.11a) ★★ Not pictured. Two faces arise from the top of *The Final Shred*'s first pitch. This route sends the steep, flat, right-side face. It is nothing special.

81. Mr. Flexible (5.11b) ★★ Not pictured. This route starts around the right side of *The Final Shred*'s block, 3 feet left of the big dead tree. Climb the arête and face for 45 feet. The crux comes about two-thirds of the way up. Use the chains at the top of *The Final Shred*'s first pitch.

77A

77B

77C

76

77

82. Chopper (5.9) ★★ Climb the crack in the dihedral. The crux comes at the small roof and flake three-quarters of the way up. This is a nice crack, but it is very fingery and can be hard to protect toward the top. Use *Mr. Flexible*'s top anchors.

83. Etched In Stone (5.10a) ★★ This is a fun, short sport route. It sends the pocketed face behind the tree and gets dirty toward the top. Climbers should be cautious of the tree in the event of a fall.

84. Oot & Aboot (5.10a) ★★ This route's bottom pitch is nice and grades ★★ for quality. Climb the fun arête to the block's top and the anchors. The crux comes about two-thirds of the way up. Toe and balance through this steep section. The second pitch is not as clean or fun and only grades ★ for quality. Continue straight up the face to the anchors at the cliff's top.

85. Stemulation (5.7) ★★ This short, little crack is set back in a dihedral. It makes an awkward climb. Jam the crack for 55 feet, then step left to the block's top.

North Talus Field

This section of the cliff has not been aggressively bolted. It has a lot of great traditional routes.

86. Johnny's Got A Gun (5.10c) ✶✶ Start right of the small fir trees. Climb the block's middle face, and tackle the bulge 20 feet up. Cruise to the chains below the big roof. The holds are slightly dirty. The route is rarely climbed.

87. Blockhead (5.9) ✶ Before the corner, a broken crack system splits the face. Jam, stem, and face climb for 30 feet. Step onto the right face, then climb 10 more feet to the top anchors next to the tree. The pushy crux comes halfway up.

88. Betaflash (5.10a) ✶✶ This route lies around the corner. Climb the arête and face 35 feet to the anchors next to the tree. The middle section is strenuous and tricky.

89. Crack Atowa (5.7) ✶✶ On the far right-side face, a crack splits the block. The rock is mossy, and the moves are nothing special. The crack flares and is hard to protect toward its top, but it still makes a decent route. Top anchors are in place.

90. Marley's Route (5.9) ✶✶ This crack lies in a dihedral of perfect red rock. Climb for 35 feet to the anchors below the roof. The crack gets thin and flares. Small pieces of protection are needed.

91. Phoups (5.10b) ★★★ The bottom flake
requires small pieces of protection. Tip jam
and stem the small dihedral for 30 feet to the
ledge and flake. Lieback through the flake
crux for 10 feet, then traverse right 10 feet to
the chains. The rock is perfect.

92. Phoups Direct (5.10d) ★ Climb the
crack system directly below *Phoups*'s anchors.
It makes a good toprope face.

93. Oregon Yosemite (5.12d) ★ This is a very strenuous, overhanging route. The flake starts with great holds. The arête's slopers are viscous, and the rock is slightly mossy.

94. Blister In The Sun (5.12c) ★★ The bottom's coarse arête is nice. This route is very strenuous and requires sequences of technical moves. The flat crux comes two-thirds of the way up. Heel hooks may come in handy.

95. Unnamed (5.11d) ★★★ This excellent route covers great rock. The short but nice arête provides great holds. The smooth crux comes toward the top.

96. Twister (5.10c) ★★★ This route has perfect rock and nice sharp holds. Traverse up and left 10 feet, then traverse up and right 25 feet to the chains. This steep route requires good footwork.

97. Eekwinocks

(5.10c) ★★ This route lies 5 feet to *Twister*'s right. Mixed climbing leads to a great hand-jam crack. The top is slightly awkward, and the bottom requires small protection.

98. Phish Food (5.11c) ★★★ Great rock and fun moves make this an excellent route. The crux comes through the route's first 20 feet. The holds get small and are not always obvious. The start has cool finger pockets.

The Final Forest

This is the cliff's final, northernmost section. There are several good tree-shaded routes in the area. This portion of the cliff does not see as much traffic as the rest.

99. Plumber Boy (5.10b) ✶✶✶ Not pictured. This sport route lies around the block's right side from *Phish Food*. The steep crux comes toward the top. The route has good holds.

100. Spring Cling (5.10a) ✶ Not pictured. This route's first hanger is gray and the rest are brown. Start behind the rotten stump in the gray buttress's middle, which is 15 feet right of *Plumber Boy*. Angle up and left to the overhang. The route splits. The left finish grades ✶✶ for quality; it keeps the route at 5.10a. The right finish grades ✶ for quality; it is 5.10b. The tree can be annoying, though the setter(s) did a good job of not overpruning.

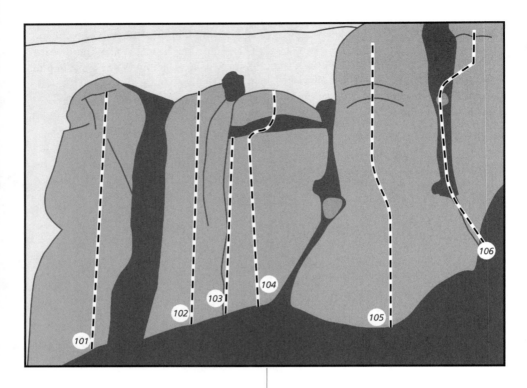

101. Spring Fever (5.9) ★★★ This route is great. Nice close bolt spacings protect the rounded ramp, and it has lots of slits and pockets. The top is a little awkward. The rock pushes one left but the bolts lead to the right.

102. Learning to Fly (5.11a) ★★ The route's bottom part is fun. The face looks craggy, but the holds are small. This is a strenuous route; it has two bulges and no great rests.

103. Lively Up Yourself (5.8) ★★ The rock is mossy, and there is a plant in the crack. This comes through the easy section, though, so it is not too bad. The crack offers fun jams and protects well. The steep crux comes through the bottom half. The crack is usually full of spider webs.

104. Special Delivery (5.9) ★★ This is a fun sport route. Climb the steep gray face. Angle up and left for 30 feet to the 3-foot overhang. Use the great holds to power through.

105. Face Lift (5.11b) ★★ This route starts on the steep brown face's middle, then moves to the left side. Climb small balancy holds through the route's middle bulge. Most climbers are pumped by the final bulge. Good holds make it possible to power through.

106. Clean Sweep (5.8) ★ This is a strange route. Start on the chimney's right side. Climb the ramp up and left to the chimney, then climb the easy chimney through the bulge. Step right onto the right-side ramp. Cruise the ramp and face to the top anchors.

MOUNT HOOD/ COLUMBIA RIVER GORGE

BULO POINT

Rock Type	Andesite
Quality of Rock (0–5)	5
Maximum Height	85 feet
Ownership	USFS

■ O V E R V I E W

Bulo Point, a wall crag of closely spaced rock pillars and boulders, is one of the best back-country climbing crags in the state. It lies on the Cascades' eastern crest and is nestled in a mature forest. Shade trees make this an excellent summer climbing area. The rocks sit at about 4,500 feet elevation. This well-developed area is host to at least twenty-eight high-quality sport and traditional climbs. Established trails exist and must be used to protect native vegetation. All routes have top anchors in place, and cracks protect well with traditional gear. The level of climbing is well suited for beginners and experts. Route grades range between 5.4 and 5.12. The solid and clean rock is sticky and makes superb climbing with lots of positive holds. A set of quick draws and a standard rack is all of the protection needed.

It takes a full week to climb all of the routes in one's grade. Climbing is possible late spring through the fall; the high altitude brings winter snow. Weather can be hot and the area is arid, so take the necessary precautions. Free camping is available off any of the nearby dirt roads, and several pay camp-grounds exist within the general area. These campgrounds have facilities such as drinking water and restrooms. The nearest camp-ground, Pebble Ford, is located 1.5 miles east of the USFS 4420 / USFS 44 junction.

Finding the crags: From Sandy, drive east on U.S. Highway 26 to Government Camp. Follow US 26 for 3 more miles to the junction with U.S. Highway 35. Turn north onto US 35 toward Hood River. From the junction, drive north for 12.6 miles and turn east onto Dufur Mill Road (USFS Road 44). Or, from Hood River, drive south on US 35 for 27 miles and turn east onto Dufur Mill Road (USFS 44).

Continue east along USFS 44 for 8.2 miles. Turn south onto paved Cold Springs Road (USFS Road 4420) toward Flag Point Lookout. Drive 0.8 mile to a gentle right curve in the road where a gravel road spurs left (straight). Turn left (straight) onto USFS Road 4421. A prominent sign reads ENTERING DUFUR CITY WATERSHED. Continue down USFS 4421 for 0.1 mile to a fork in the road. Stay to the right, turning onto

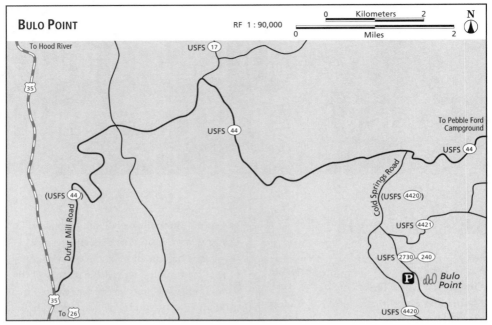

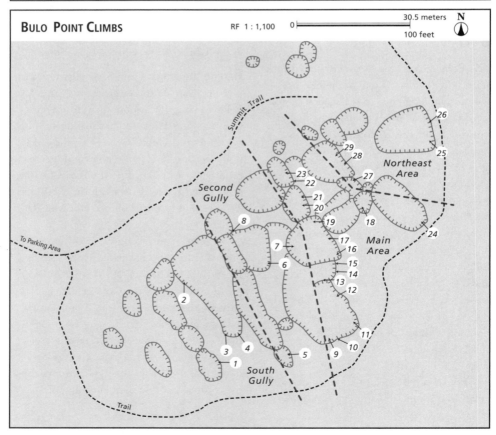

Bulo Point is an excellent backcountry climbing crag with a must-see view from the top.

USFS Road 2730-240, and drive exactly 1 mile from this junction. Park in a pullout on either side of the road. A good trail leads east to the rocks. Hike approximately 150 yards downhill to the cliff's base.

South Gully

This is the first gully one encounters hiking down the trail to the cliff's bottom. It has several good routes.

1. Silence of the Cams (5.7) ★★★ This route lies on the south-side entrance of the

first gully. It is well protected and makes a good warm-up climb. Climb the broken face past three bolts to the top-chains. It is steep and pushy but has great handholds.

2. Inversion Excursion (5.8) ★★ This route lies at the gully's top on the north-side wall. Climb the crack and faces to a ledge below the first bolt; this section can be supplemented with traditional protection. Step right to a flake, then climb the ramp-face past several bolts to the top anchors. The top anchors do not have chains, so a walk-off is necessary. The balancy crux comes between the first and second bolts.

3. Drawin' a Blank (5.12a) ★★ This route shares the first bolt and top-chains with *Separated at Birth*. It tackles the large ceiling's left side. Climb the ramp on solid holds to the large overhang. The powerful crux is a series of difficult moves on mediocre holds between the second and fourth bolts. Pull over the ceiling's left side, and climb a strenuous overhanging face to a small ledge. Step left and tackle an overhanging bulge (5.10). Climb through to the top-chains.

4. Separated at Birth (5.10b) ★★★ Climb the ceiling's right side, and squeeze through a shallow chimney to a pleasant face. The 5.8 start has good holds to pull through the overhang. The difficult crux comes at the route's top. Climb over the overhanging bulge on sloping handholds to the top-chains.

Second Gully

The Second Gully is easily identified by the large chockstone toward its entrance. The upper routes can be accessed by rappelling from the cliff's top or by scrambling upward from the gully's bottom.

5. Atomic Dust Buster (5.11a) ✯✯ This climb sends the steep overhanging face situated at the second gully's entrance. The first bolt is fairly high; a clip-stick is recommended. The crux comes between the first and second bolts. Climb the overhanging face past several bolts to the rock's top. Walk off the rock's backside.

6. Barking Spider

(5.6) ✯✯ Start on the ledge at the gully's top. This route sends a chunky spine to the cliff's top. Abundant large handholds and footholds take one past several bolts to the top anchors. Lower down or walk off the top.

7. Slice of Pie (5.8) ✯ Climb the crack in the gully's upper portion opposite *Barking Spider*. One- to 4-inch traditional protection is required. Bolts without chains are on the route's awkward and mossy top. Bring webbing and rings to rappel off of, or climb an exposed face to the cliff's top.

8. Wood Fur (5.4) ✯ Not pictured. This route is most easily accessed by hiking to the cliff's top. It lies in a small gully with a broken-top dead tree. Oversize protection is needed to protect the large crack, and a toprope is recommended. Top-bolts are in place. Climb and stem off large holds on both sides of the off-width crack. This nonintimidating short climb makes a good beginner route.

The Main Area

The main climbing area is home to the best routes at Bulo Point. Its bottom portion is often shaded and has large flat belay areas. Descending from the cliff's top is the best way to access the Main Area's top portion, in the upper gully. This includes Routes 19 through 23. Downclimb 10 feet of 5th-class rock to a large rock ledge. Belay and climb the upper routes from this large ledge.

9. For the Love of God Alice Shut the Bathroom Door (5.10a) ✭✭✭ This splendid route sends perfect rock. It used to follow the crack system to the left of the top bulge, but was recently bolted and now tackles the top bulge head on. Climb the easy ramp-face past several bolts to the top bulge. Make an exciting long lock-off balancing on small footholds to a large handhold. Climb through to the top-chains.

10. J-Rat Crack (5.7) ✭ Climb the wide crack up the rock's middle section. The awkward crux comes at the small ceiling. Use medium to large traditional gear to protect the crack. The route shares top-chains with *Raiders of the Lost Rock*.

11. Raiders of the Lost Rock (5.9) ✭✭
Climb large holds up easy rock to a flake and small bulge. The route's first bolt is 15 feet off the ground. Supplement with traditional gear if necessary. Move through the balancy crux to the ramp-face, then climb the fun face to the top-chains.

Shared Anchor

12

13

12. I Am Not the Man (5.12+) ★★ This blank face was recently bolted. Climb solid holds to the first bolt. The crux comes through a series of balancy fingerholds with micro-footholds on the steep face. The second clip is very difficult to make. Above the second bolt, climb large holds to the top-chains.

13. Plumbers Crack (5.5) ★★ Climb the easy crack system inside the dihedral to its end. Traverse left to the top-chains shared with *I Am Not the Man*. This crack system protects well with medium to large traditional gear.

14. Return of Yoda (5.10c) ★★★ This sport climb sends great rock. Climb large holds up the ramp-face past several bolts to a bulge at the route's top. The crux comes at the fourth bolt. Make a series of balancy moves on pushy and insecure holds through the bulge to the top-chains.

15. Nook and Cranny (5.7) ★★★ This fantastic traditional route protects well with small to medium gear. It climbs the crack system on the face's right side. Make a series of enjoyable moves to the thin crux at the route's top. Stem and use powerful hand jams to climb through to the top anchors.

16. Jet Stream
(5.9) ★★★ This excellent, tall sport route sends the airy spine on the face's left side. An area classic and the most popular route at Bulo Point, it

climbs positive holds with intimidating exposure on perfect rock. The bolt spaces are nice and close.

17. Jet Wind (5.8) ★★★ This area classic is the second-best route in the crag next to *Jet Stream*. Start at the base of *Jet Stream*. At the first bolt, climb up and right. Follow a series of closely spaced bolts on secure holds with airy exposure. The route's middle section is steep and sustained. Continue to the rock's top and top-chains. This well-protected route makes an excellent lead climb and is highly recommended.

18. Black Market Organ Donor (5.10a) ★★
This long route sends the spine to the right
of *Jet Stream*. It is a mixed route requiring 1-
to 4-inch traditional gear for supplemental
protection, as there are two 20-foot bolt
spaces. Start on the spine's left side. At the
first bolt, make an awkward traverse to the
right-side face. Continue climbing up large
holds and positive cracks to a bird's nest and
overhanging bulge. Surmounting this bulge is
the route's crux. Make a balancy move with
mediocre handholds to surmount the small
overhanging bulge, then climb the easy ramp
to the top-chains.

19. Climbs With a Fist (5.9) ★★ Descend from the cliff's top to a large rock ledge at the route's bottom. This route sends the far right-side face and lies 10 feet to the right of *Jet Wind*'s upper half. Climb past a series of bolts on solid rock to the route's top-chains. Because of its location, it sees far fewer ascents than the other routes in the Main Area. The technical crux lies toward the route's top.

20. Nuke the Gay Whales for Jesus (5.7) ★★★ Climb the bolted arête on the block's left edge. The crux comes at the route's start. An abundance of good holds makes this a fun route with airy exposure.

21. Cattle Guard (5.9) ★★★ Start with a series of long lock-offs on positive holds. This fun route sends perfect rock. The route is steep and does not provide a good rest until over halfway up. The crux comes through the route's middle section and consists of a series of sustained 5.8+ moves. Continue up the solid face to the top-chains.

22. Bulo Dancing (5.7) ✭✭ This route follows the large off-width crack splitting the two large blocks. It can be protected with oversize traditional gear but makes a better toprope climb. Climb large face holds through a small bulge. Stem and climb both faces until the crack becomes too wide. Step right and climb the face to the top-chains. The crux comes toward the route's top.

23. Line Dancing (5.8) ✭✭ Climb the 1-inch crack splitting the block's face. Small to medium traditional gear is needed to protect the crack. The steep crux comes at the route's middle section. Climb through on secure but delicate holds. The crack's top portion provides fun and secure hand jams.

24. Don't Call Me Ishmael (5.11b) ★★
Climb the short but aggressively overhanging face. The spacing between the second and third bolts is long; use extra caution. Power through a series of good holds to a long lock-off above the second bolt. Snare the flake crack, then power through the final bulge to the top-chains.

Northeast Section

The Northeast Section has routes on a large block that are accessed from the bottom trail, as well as routes in the upper gully that are best accessed by rappelling from the cliff's top.

25. Scene of the Crime (5.10b) ✶✶✶

Tackle the large ceiling's left side. Climb the ramp, then step right under the overhang. Power through this steep crux on good holds, then climb great holds up the face to the route's top. This route shares top-chains with *DaKind*.

26. DaKind (5.9) ✶✶✶ This splendid mixed route sends the large ceiling's right side. The crux comes through the overhanging ceiling at the route's start. Heel hook and power through to an enjoyable sustained 5.7 face. Use traditional gear to protect the route's start, or use a clip-stick to set the first bolt.

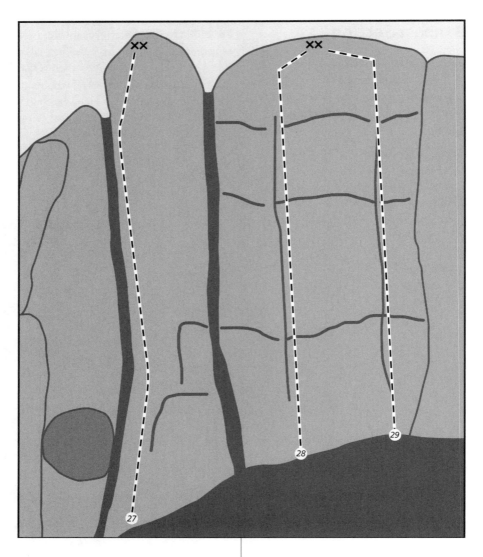

27. Who's the Choss? (5.7) A 5-foot-wide face is created by two parallel cracks. Climb the mossy face and left-side crack. At the crack's top, step right and climb the face to the top anchors. This exposed and airy step is the route's crux. The rock is loose and mossy, and the crack is filled with dirt and vegetation. This route is not recommended.

28. Rock Thugs in Harmony (5.9) ★★ This route sends the upper gully's left-side face.

Climb solid holds on mediocre rock past several bolts to the top anchors. The rock on the route's bottom portion is dirty and mossy, but the rock quality increases toward the top.

29. Cam Digger (5.7) ★ This mundane traditional route shares top anchors with *Rock Thugs in Harmony*. Climb the bushy and dirty crack on the right-side face. Protect the crack with medium-size traditional gear.

PETE'S PILE

Rock Type	Basalt
Quality of Rock (0–5)	4
Maximum Height	200 feet
Ownership	USFS

◼ O V E R V I E W

Pete's Pile is a well-developed climbing area nestled within a columnar basalt cliff ban. It lies in a mature forest overlooking Mount Hood's east side and has several single-pitch and a few multi-pitch traditional-style routes. There are currently sixteen documented routes, several more nondocumented ones, and potential for dozens more. The area is well developed with trails, signs, level belays, and top anchors in place on all routes. The climbing level ranges from beginner to intermediate; route grades range from 5.6 to 5.10a. The rock is clean and solid and protects well. A standard rack of traditional gear is needed. These are tall, sustained routes. The area provides for several days of climbing. Climbing is best late spring through fall; winters are wet. This west-facing cliff is shady in the morning and sunny in the afternoon. The middle section of Pete's Pile is closed to climbing for protection of a rare plant species. Notice and follow access signs. Services such as drinking water and restrooms are available at Sherwood Campground, 0.6 mile south on Highway 35. Free camping is available off USFS Road 44.

Finding the crags: From Hood River, take Interstate 84 exit 64 to Highway 35. Drive south on Highway 35 toward Government Camp for 23 miles. Park in the large paved pullout 0.3 mile past mile marker 73. The cliff lies 150 yards up the hill on the road's east side.

The trailhead lies at the beginning of the overgrown, paved spur road. Hike the steep trail uphill for 0.8 mile to Pete's Pile, following the signs along the trail. To access the cliff's base, stay left at the fork 300 yards up the trail. To hike to the cliff's top, turn right at the fork in the trail. From the fork, hike 50 yards to a 15-foot 4th-class scramble to the cliff's top. Signs guide the way. Topropes can be set for some routes.
Warning: Access to most top anchors is very exposed. Use extreme caution.

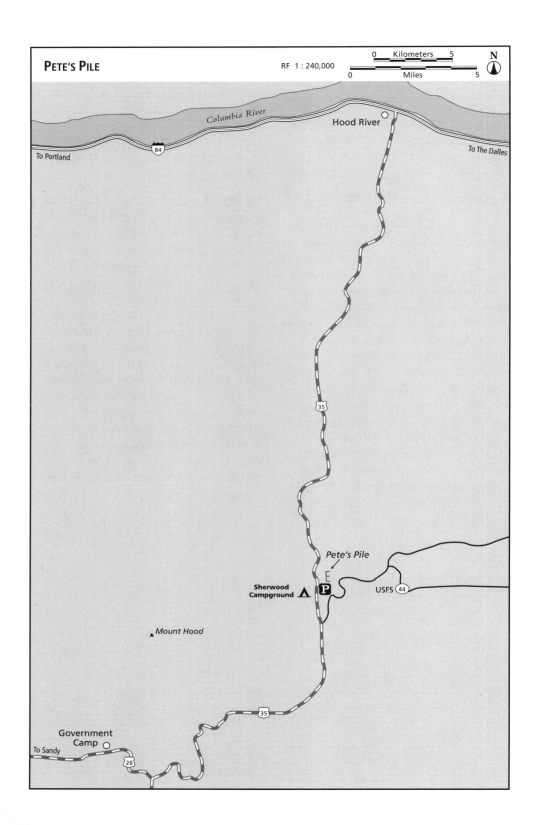

PETE'S PILE CLIMBING AREAS

RF 1 : 1,100

45.7 meters

N

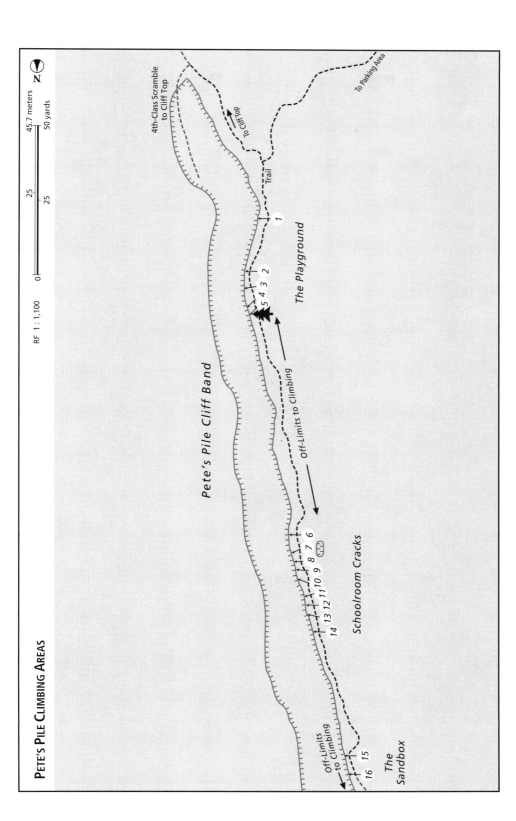

4th-Class Scramble to Cliff Top

To Cliff Top

To Parking Area

Trail

Pete's Pile Cliff Band

The Playground

Off-Limits to Climbing

Schoolroom Cracks

Off-Limits to Climbing

The Sandbox

Pete's Pile is a tall cliff cloaked in a mature forest with a panorama of Mount Hood's east side.

The Playground

This is the first grouping of routes encountered from the trailhead, and all of them are excellent climbs. These are tall routes; a 60-meter rope is needed. This is the only area where topropes can be set for some routes via the cliff's top, but the top is exposed and this action is not encouraged. The NO CLIMBING ZONE sign establishes the area's north-side boundary.

1. Beer Garden (5.8) ★★ This is the first route encountered as one approaches the Playground. It sits alone and lies 20 feet right of the main route grouping. A wood log creates a small, level belay area. Climb the fun and easy ramp to a small ceiling and pull over the top. Climb the cracks and pushy flat walls to the cliff's top. The top section is sustained 5.8. The crux comes two-thirds of the way up the route. This is a tall route, and a 60-meter rope is necessary for a lowered descent. The route's top anchors are set back 5 feet from the cliff's edge.

2. For Pete's Sake (5.8) ★★★ This splendid route protects well. Climb fun, blocky holds for 30 feet to a small roof and flat face. This is the crux. Use the crack to pull over the roof, then climb the fun and easy crack to the cliff's top and the top-chains.

3. Guillotine (5.10a) ★★★ Climb the mixed route to a 2-foot ceiling 45 feet up. This is the guillotine. The technical crux comes just above this ceiling. The route pro- tects well but requires small protection; a standard rack of nuts provides the correct size. Climb the solid crack above the ceiling to the top-chains.

4. Temptation (5.9) ✮✮✮ This is an excellent route, even though the start is bushy. The crux comes through a 15-foot 5.9 sustained section above the 12-inch triangle-shaped ceiling 20 feet up. The route's upper portion is more difficult to protect and slightly runout in sections, but is easier climbing on bomber holds. A few loose rocks lie toward the route's top. The top-chains lie directly above the route, which can also be toproped by accessing the bolts 6 feet right of the route from the cliff's top.

5. Even (5.7) ✯✯✯ This is an excellent climb and an area classic. It starts 4 feet right of a large fir tree growing at the cliff's base. The crux lies 20 feet up through the flat walls and thin cracks, and the route's grade drops to 5.6 beyond it. The route protects well with large to small gear, and top-chains are in place.

Schoolroom Cracks

Schoolroom Cracks, the middle grouping of routes, is the most heavily accessed section of the cliff. There are several great routes and a bench to belay from. Hike 60 yards north, past the Playground, to access the area.

6. Bottlecap (5.10a) ★★ This route's name comes from the large bottle cap–shaped ceiling 30 feet up. It lies 20 feet right of the bench behind a tall fir tree. Climb 30 feet to the large 3-foot ceiling, then move right of the ceiling onto the rock's face. Climb the crack another 40 feet to the top-chains. Several annoying bushes lie in the crack's upper portion.

7. Smokin' In the Boys Room (5.8) ✶✶✶
This splendid route is fairly sustained and
covers solid rock and great holds. The crack
protects well with small to medium gear. The
crux lies two-thirds of the way up, where the
left wall is void of features.

8. Hot For Teacher (5.9) ✶✶ Climb the
crack in the open book while stemming the
two faces. The sustained crux lies halfway up.
Climb through the balancy crux for 10 feet,
then send easier rock to the route's top-
chains. The route's protection is solid, but the
best placements are spaced far apart.

9. Schoolroom (5.9) ✶✶
Climb the crack to the
top-chains by stemming

the small holds on both walls. The sustained
crux comes two-thirds of the way up. The
route's top half is more difficult to protect;
the most solid placements are spaced farther
apart. The route shares top anchors with *Hot
For Teacher.*

10. Dunce (5.6) ✶✶ This is the leftmost of
the four closely spaced routes. The entire
route is sustained 5.6, but the technical crux
comes at the small ceiling. The route protects
well with medium to large gear. Jam and
stem the crack, then step right at the top to
the route's top-chains.

11. Unknown This route sends the line two cracks right of *Escalade*. It is mossy and dirty and needs to be cleaned. Climb 20 feet to a large ceiling. Step left, then climb the crack 40 feet and step left again to the top-chains. The route's name, difficulty grade, and quality grade are unknown.

12. Escalade (5.7) ★★ This incredibly fun route protects well and may be the best in the area despite seeing fewer ascents. Start in the overhanging crack on the detached block's right side, and climb up to the overhang. Step out on the block's face to surmount the feature. Ground-fall potential exists through the route's start unless one has extra-large gear to use, but the easy climbing and huge holds mitigate the risk. Climb the crack in the dihedral to the top-chains. The crux comes at the steep bulge near the route's top.

13. Ramble On (5.7R) ★★ This route is still dirty and sees less action than most of the others, though it does have potential. Its bottom is very runout; extreme caution or avoidance is advised. Climb the ramp to the right-side crack in the dihedral. The route protects better once reaching the crack. The crux comes through the smooth bulge 10 feet above the large ceiling. Continue in the right-side dihedral to the top, then traverse up and left to the top-chains.

14. Pumpin For the Man (5.9+) ★★ This route's third pitch is airy, exposed, and exciting. Unfortunately, one must climb two mediocre pitches to access it. The route is close to 200 feet tall and climbs to the cliff's top. Walk down from the cliff's top. Hike south for 200 yards and downclimb the 4th-class scramble to the cliff's base. **Pitch 1:** (5.9) Start under the left side of a steep chimney. Pull up and climb a few feet to the large ceiling, then traverse right to the crack in the open book. Beware of rope drag if protection is used within the first 10 feet. Climb the crack for 60 feet, passing a small ceiling. At the 2-foot ceiling, step left to anchors and the first belay. There are some very large loose blocks below the belay; climbers below need be extremely cautious. The crux comes below the small ceiling halfway up. **Pitch 2:** (5.8) From the belay, climb up and right to the crack. Continue over or around the 2-foot ceiling, then climb the crack 25 feet to a large ledge.

From the ledge, climb the off-width crack created by the detached pillar to its top. This is the second belay ledge, and it sits left of a large 6-foot ceiling. Anchors are in place. The pitch's top half is easy but is difficult to protect without extra-large gear. The technical crux comes at the start of the pitch. **Pitch 3:** (5.9) From the belay ledge, work up and right to the right-side crack. This is a tall and sustained 90-foot pitch. Jam and stem the strenuous crack and flat walls to the cliff's top and the top-chains. The crux comes at the smooth, steep bulge two-thirds of the way up. This is an airy and exciting pitch.

The Sandbox

The Sandbox lies at Pete's Pile's very north end, approximately 70 yards north of Schoolroom Cracks. There are currently only two routes here. The cliff to the north of the OUTER LIMITS sign is closed to climbing.

15. Dunlap (5.9) ★★ Climb the flat face between two parallel cracks. Focus on the left-side crack as it protects better. This fun route protects well but is still a little dirty. The steep crux comes through the flat section a little over halfway up. Make a series of sustained 5.9 moves until reaching easier holds toward the route's top.

16. Outer Limits (5.10a) ★★ This is the farthest-left route at Pete's Pile. Start right of the stacked, leaning blocks. Climb the easy crack on the block's right side to the steep wall above. Jam the crack, and balance on small edges to the top-chains. The crack is still mossy and dirty, and it holds a few plants. This route has great potential once it is adequately cleaned. It protects well with a standard rack. The crux comes through the middle section of the flat wall above the leaning blocks.

FRENCH'S DOME

Rock Type	Volcanic
Quality of Rock (0–5)	4
Maximum Height	150 feet
Ownership	USFS

■ OVERVIEW

French's Dome is host to a number of high-quality sport routes. The level of climbing ranges from beginner to expert. Climbs are graded between 5.6 and 5.13+, and it takes several days to climb all of the routes in one's grade. The area is well developed and popular. There are good trails, bolts, and leveled belay areas. The climbing season starts in early summer and continues through late fall, but snow blocks access during the winter. The rock is sticky and covered in edges. Lack of holds is rarely a problem—although the size of the holds can be. The dome lies in a mature forest and is continually shaded. Do not hike off of or make new trails. Free camping is available off many of the nearby gravel roads; drinking water and restrooms are not.

Finding the crags: Follow U.S. Highway 26 east from Sandy for 17 miles. At mile marker 42, turn north onto Lolo Pass Road (USFS Road 18). The road lies on the edge of Zigzag, just after the ranger station. Drive 6 miles to the trailhead parking area, a dirt pullout in a clear-cut on the right side of the road. The trail starts on the parking area's northeast side. It descends the hill into the timber; follow it 250 feet to the dome.

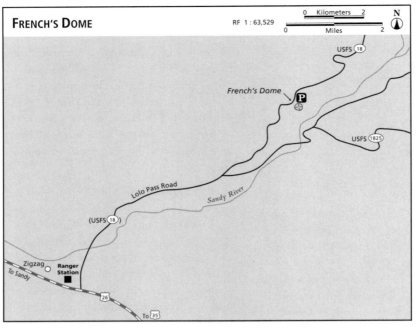

FRENCH'S DOME

RF 1 : 63,529

0 Kilometers 2
0 Miles 2

N

USFS 18

French's Dome P

USFS 1825

Lolo Pass Road

Sandy River

(USFS 18)

Zigzag
To Sandy
Ranger Station

26

To 35

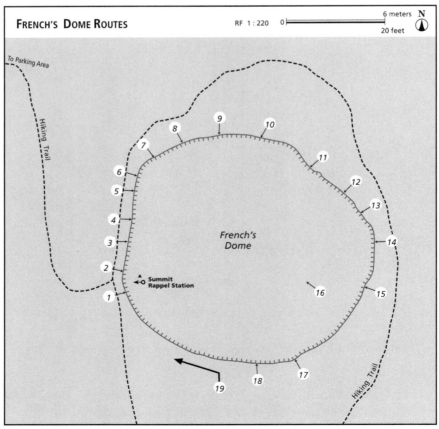

FRENCH'S DOME ROUTES

RF 1 : 220

0 6 meters
20 feet

N

To Parking Area

Hiking Trail

7
8
9
10
6
5
11
4
12
3
13
2
Summit Rappel Station
French's Dome
14
1
16
15
17
18
19

Hiking Trail

French's Dome is easily accessible from the road and lies within a scenic forest on Mount Hood's west side.

French's Dome

1. High Voltage (5.12b/c) ★★★ This is the first route encountered when approaching the rock from the trail. It starts 2 feet to the trail's right and is relatively new. The route follows a steep face with tiny edges, then tackles a large bulge.

2. Road Face (5.12b) ★★ This route is an area classic. It originally rated 5.4, A3, but has since been retro-bolted and is now a good sport climb. The constant overhanging face is a test of endurance.

3. Unknown (5.13+/5.14-?) ★★ This difficult route combines a bouldery start with a flat, overhanging face. The route has seen few redpoints. A right-side variation starts 10 feet to the right of the original route.

4. Unknown (5.13+?) A new bolted line appears 10 feet right of *China Syndrome*. This overhanging face hosts only small holds, making it a difficult line.

5. China Syndrome, aka China Man (5.11b) ★★★ This is a highly favored area classic.

The route offers fluid moves up a gently overhanging face. Holds are plentiful. The slight overhang adds a lot of difficulty over the route's length.

6. Siege (5.13) ★★★ This route's bouldery crux comes through the first 20 feet. The bottom is extremely technical. The small holds are spaced far apart; perfect balance is needed. The difficulty lets up after the fifth bolt.

7. Pump-O-Rama (5.12b) ★★ Not pictured. This route sends the black streak of overhanging rock. The bottom is very difficult. The entire route is overhanging and a test of one's endurance. There are good holds, even though some require long lock-offs. There are no good rests until two-thirds of the way up.

8. Crankenstein (5.11c) ★★★ Not pictured. This one is straightforward. Climb the long, steep wall to the top anchors. The first crux (11-) comes between the fourth and fifth bolts. The second and technical crux comes at the steep bulge at the route's top.

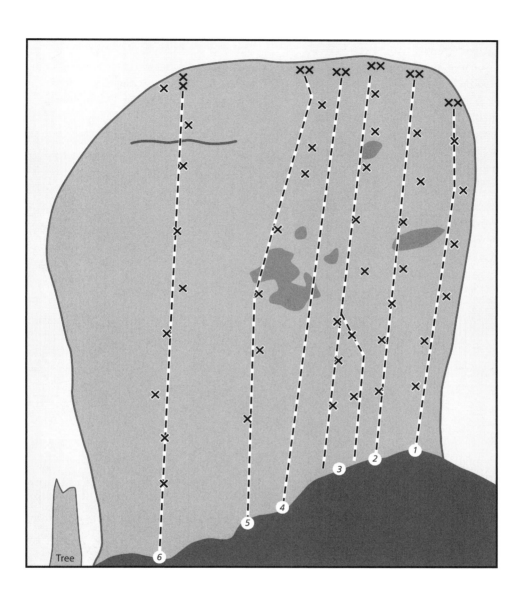

Tree

9. Silver Streak (5.10b) ✭✭✭ Start by climbing up the nice, easy ramp, then tackle the steep wall above. The rock is solid and clean, and the moves are fluid. There are good holds, but the route's steepness adds a lot of difficulty. The crux comes at the bulge near the fourth bolt.

10. Straw Man (5.8) ✭✭✭ Climb the steep face to the first bolt, then continue on easy rock and solid holds to the steep crux at the fifth bolt. Balance through and continue on to the top-chains. The bolt spacings are close, and the rock is clean and solid. This route is an area classic.

11. Alpha Centauri (5.8) ★★★ Start by climbing up an easy, solid gully. Send the shallow bulge, then follow the ramp-face to the steep but easy top. The holds toward the route's top are incredibly positive, making this a really fun route. The crux comes at the fourth bolt.

12. Emerald City (5.8) ★★★ This relatively new route is easily identified by its shiny bolts. Climb an easy ramp to the steep face, where the crux comes through the face at the fourth bolt. There are always good holds, but they must be patiently searched out. Continue on good rock, through to the top's fun chunky section to the top-chains.

13. Tin Man (5.7) ★★★ This route sends solid rock, but the bolt spacings are a little intimidating. It shares the start and first bolt with *The Americas*. At the first bolt, climb up and right, then climb to the right side of the blocky spine. The crux lies at the third bolt. At the spine's top, step left and join *The Americas* to the top-chains.

14. The Americas (5.6) ★★★ This excellent beginner route is very popular. Start in the gully, and climb large ledges up the blocky spine to the top anchors.

15. Giant's Staircase (5.6) ★ This is the first route to the dome's summit and is often referred to as the Pioneer Route. The three-pitch route is close to 150 feet tall and is popular. Start on the rock's east side. The dome's summit must be rappelled from. A rappel station lies on the rock's west side, directly over the entrance trail. Be sure to call below for climbers before throwing a rope over the rock's edge. **Pitch 1:** (5.6) Climb large blocks in an easy gully past three bolts. Continue up and left to belay chains on a large ledge. **Pitch 2:** (5.5) From the belay, traverse right, avoiding a 15-foot vertical wall above the belay. Continue traversing around a small ridge. Climb upward to an easy right traverse to a cleaner gully, then climb straight up this gully past a bolt to a bolted belay. The second pitch is sparsely protected. **Pitch 3:**

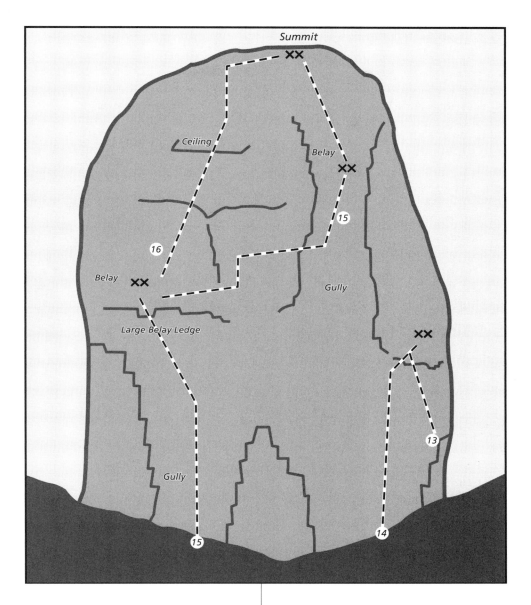

(5.1) From the belay, scramble up the gully to French's Dome's summit, where there are two bolts spaced about 5 feet apart. Long runners make these easier to belay from. Rappel from the rappel station on the rock's west side, directly above the entrance trail.

16. Static Cling (5.9) ✷✷ This is a variation to reach the rock's summit from the top of

Giant's Staircase's first pitch. Send the bolt line directly above the first belay. Balance past three bolts to easier climbing, and continue on to a 2-foot ceiling. This is the crux. Tackle the ceiling, then scramble easier rock to the dome's summit. Rappel the dome from the rappel station on the rock's west side, directly above the entrance trail.

17. Low Voltage (5.11a) ✱✱✱ This great route is well protected and sends excellent rock. It lies by itself, tucked away on the dome's southeast side. Climb the steep overhanging face past five bolts. Step right onto the ramp-face, and continue past one more bolt to the top-chains. A 5.10+ lower crux sends the sloping holds above the second bolt. The technical and true crux comes at the fourth bolt. Positive holds exist, but the overhang is strenuous.

18. Unknown (5.14?) Two top anchors and a rope-setting bolt lie on this blank face. No beta could be found for the impossible-looking face.

19. Yellow Brick Road (5.8 R) ✱ Not pictured. This is the only traditional route at the crag, and it is rarely climbed. A ramp of large blocks winds up the dome's south side. Start near the ramp's bottom. Climb the steep face to a bolt, then move onto the ramp and continue up it till its end. Climb straight up 15 feet of exposed, steep rock to the wall's top. The rock is mossy, and protection can be suspect. This route is not recommended.

SALMON RIVER SLAB

Rock Type	Volcanic
Quality of Rock (0–5)	3
Maximum Height	50 feet
Ownership	USFS

■ OVERVIEW

Salmon River Slab is a steep slab next to the Salmon River. It has several sport routes and is well developed. The bolts are solid and closely spaced, and all routes have top anchors in place. A large pullout next to the rock provides easy parking. The level of climbing ranges from beginner to intermediate; route grades range from 5.5 to 5.9. Given the grades and superior protection, this crag is well suited for beginning rock climbers. The rock is solid with minimal moss but stays damp during the spring. Evidence of dynamite-blasting holes suggests portions of the original rock were removed during road construction, leaving the slab as it is today. This type of granular rock has lots of positive holds and is sticky. A set of quick draws is all the gear that is needed.

It takes one day to climb all of the routes. Climbing is best late spring through fall; winters are wet and there is often snow. The slab is west-facing, so it is shaded in the morning and sun-drenched in the afternoon. Directly across the road from the slab is a great swimming hole in the Salmon River. Few logging roads spur from the main road; consequently, camping is mostly limited to one of several nearby pay-campgrounds. Services such as drinking water and restrooms are available at Green Canyons Campground, 0.5 mile south of the slab.

Finding the crags: From Sandy, drive east on U.S. Highway 26 for 15 miles to Zigzag. Entering Zigzag, turn south onto Salmon River Road (USFS Road 2618) and drive 3.9 miles. Park in an obvious pullout next to the rock slab. The obvious rock lies to the road's east side and is difficult to miss.

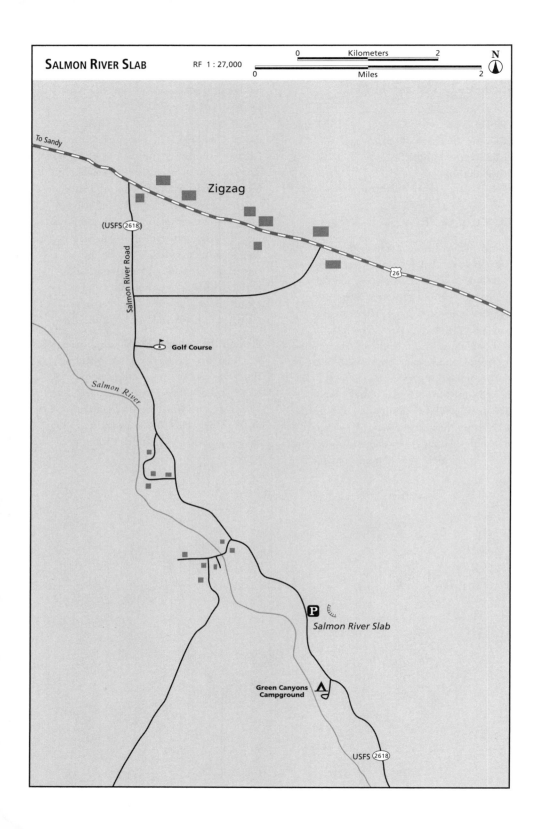

Salmon River Slab is a solid rock cliff conveniently located right off the road.

Salmon River Slab

1. Climbing Theme (5.6) ✷ This is the far-thest-left route on the slab. Large positive holds lead past several closely spaced bolts to top anchors. It is a fun and enjoyable route, and would be a superior one, except that several sections of loose rock significantly degrade its quality. The crux comes above the third bolt.

2. White and Brown Rice (5.8) ✷✷✷ Balance and climb on small but positive ledges past several bolts to the top anchors. The rock is solid, and the holds are clean. This is the best route at the crag. Precision footwork is necessary. The crux comes at the small ceiling toward the route's top.

3. Camel Back (5.9) ✷✷ Climb alternating between small balancy edges and large posi-tive holds, through several steep bulges to the

route's top anchors. This is a good route that sends solid rock and is well protected. There are two 5.8+ cruxes. The first is at the route's start, and the second is below the second-to-the-last bolt.

4. Cave Man Crawl (5.7) ✷✷ This route has a steep start, but large positive holds make it relatively easy. Climb through the start's right side, then climb the shallow ramp past sev-eral bolts to the top anchors. A moderate level of ground-fall potential exists at the second bolt. Though it is easy, a clip-stick is recommended.

5. Stinky Salmon (5.5) ✷ This route trav-erses over the steep arch on the wall's right side. Follow bolts up and left over the steep arch, then climb easy rock past several bolts to the route's top-chains. Some sections of rock are loose and dirty.

HARLAN WALL

Rock Type	Lava
Quality of Rock (0–5)	2
Maximum Height	70 feet
Ownership	Private

■ OVERVIEW

Harlan Wall is nestled in a roadside quarry and provides limited sport climbing. All of the routes are bolted; some of the bolts are missing or are spaced far apart. The climbing level ranges from beginner to intermediate, with all routes grading 5.10 or below. The rock is edgy lava and is fairly solid, but loose sections exist. Some portions of the wall are covered in moss and grass. It takes a day to climb all of the routes. The low altitude permits year-round access, though the rock is often wet during winter and spring. Shade trees and its proximity to Elk Creek make this a nice crag to visit during summer months. Be cautious of rockfall toward the wall's right side. Small amounts of poison oak are present, so take the necessary precautions. Harlan Wall is private property. Access to the area is currently permitted, but this could change at any time in the future. Look for and obey access signs. Please treat the area with respect and help keep it clean. Users of this area are solely responsible for their own safety; the property owners are in no way liable for users' actions or consequences. Camping is available at nearby Big Elk Campground, which has limited facilities such as drinking water and restrooms.

Finding the crags: Follow U.S. Highway 20 west from Corvallis for 18.8 miles. At

HARLAN WALL

RF 1 : 161,000

0   Kilometers   2
0   Miles   2

N

To Toledo and Newport

20

Burnt Woods Store

To Corvallis

Harlan Burnt Woods Road

Shotpouch Road

Harlan Road

Harlan Wall

Big Elk Campground

Old Harlan Store

Grant Creek Road

Marys Peak Road

Harlan Wall is a small roadside quarry with a nice selection of moderate routes.

mile marker 33, turn left (south) onto Harlan Burnt Woods Road, just after the Burnt Woods Store. Continue for 7.7 miles to the junction with Harlan Road; the Old Harlan Store is at this intersection. Turn right onto gravel Harlan Road and follow it for 2.3 miles to Harlan Wall, which is on the road's right (north) side. Park in the pullout next to the wall.

Harlan Wall

1. Clip It (5.6) ✴✴✴ Climb past two solid bolts to a large ledge, then climb through a series of large ledges to the top anchors. The crux comes at the fourth bolt. The bolts are closely spaced, making this a good lead climb for beginners. The rock is solid and fairly clean.

2. Squamish (5.8) ✴ *Squamish* and *Scratch It* share the same first bolt. Climb past one bolt to a large ledge, then step left to the next bolt. Continue up and left past four more bolts to the anchors on the cliff's top. The middle ledge is dirty and grassy.

3. Scratch It (5.8) ✴✴ At the first bolt, move up and right past two large ledges. Climb the solid crack and face to the top-chains. This route has an exciting start.

4. Kamakazee (5.10a) ★★★ This is an area classic. Start between the two maple trees, and follow the bolted crack through several overhangs and ceilings. Each overhang has good holds to power through. The crux comes at the fourth bolt. Continue up and right to the top-chains. A few annoying plants are in the upper crack. The second-to-the-last bolt is runout. A 2-inch cam is recommended.

5. Shortstack (5.10a) The rock quality and protection in this route's middle and upper portions are suspect. Climb the fun and solid face past three bolts to a large ledge; this route would be better if it stopped here.

Climb through alternating sections of solid and questionable rock to the top anchors 20 feet below the cliff's top. This is a tall route— 70 feet. The crux comes through the route's bottom section.

HIGHWAY 11

Rock Type	Volcanic
Quality of Rock (0–5)	1
Maximum Height	60 feet
Ownership	Private/BLM

■ O V E R V I E W

The Highway 11 area offers limited sport climbing. The technical difficulty of the routes makes them best suited for beginners, but intermediate climbing experience is recommended. Routes grade between 5.5 and 5.8. Most are runout and much of the fixed protection is old and should not be trusted. The rock's quality is too poor to support difficult routes; most of it is loose and dirty. It takes two days to climb all of the routes. Winter and spring are very wet; climbing is best summer through fall. Green Peter Lake can provide relief from the summer's heat. The few sections of solid rock are sticky and covered with good edges. The Main Wall is 10 feet off the road, so traffic is common. Take the necessary precautions. Free and pay camping sites are available along Highway 11. Camping is allowed at Sunnyside County Park at the northeast end of Foster Reservoir, at Whitcomb Creek County Park located south of Highway 11 between the climbing wall and the Pillar, and at Yellowbottom Campground farther north on Highway 11.

Finding the crags: Follow U.S. Highway 20 east from Sweet Home for 2 miles. Just before mile marker 33, turn north onto Quartzville Drive, which eventually turns into USFS Road 11. Drive 5 miles to the Main Wall, located on the east side of the road 0.25 mile after the dam. Drive another 7 miles to reach the Pillar, which is 0.25 mile before mile marker 13, directly above the west end of a wall of semisolid rock.

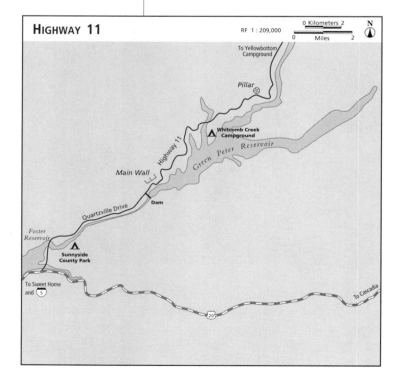

Easy access and relatively low technical difficulty make Highway 11 a great place for intermediate-level climbers.

Main Wall

The Main Wall lies on private property, owned by a timber company. Access is currently allowed but may be closed off at any time. Watch for signs restricting access.

The main wall has six sport climbs. Fixed protection that appears old or weak should not be trusted. The rock is dirty and loose; take the necessary precautions. It is recommended to toprope the routes and check all fixed protection before leading them.

1. Timid (5.7 X) Not pictured. This route ascends the far left side of the main wall. Climb the bulging ramp and clip the single bolt. Finish by climbing the solid top. This route is easy but very runout. Top anchors are not in place, and one must hike down from the top. Use a cam to protect the crack below the bolt.

2. The Zone (5.6 R) The first bolt is runout. The rock is dirty and rotten; study the route before climbing it. It is not recommended.

3. Crazy James (5.6) This route is dirty and loose. Fixed protection should not be trusted. Weave back and forth to stay on the cleanest, most solid rock.

4. Kamikaze (5.7) ★ This route and *Crazy James* share the same start. Weave back and forth to stay on the cleanest, most solid rock. Check the holds before pulling on them. This exciting route is the wall's best one.

5. Bad Tendencies (5.5 R) ✶ This route is runout; three bolts protect its entire length. Be cautious of loose rock, and follow the cleanest path possible. This is the second-best route on the Main Wall.

6. Freddie's Streak (5.7 R) This route is runout; three bolts protect its entire length. Be cautious of loose rock. The crux comes at the route's bottom. The top anchors lie to the right of the bush.

Highway 11 Pillar

The Pillar lies on public, BLM land. The rock is more solid than the Main Wall's. Most of the Pillar is covered with moss. The summit offers a pleasant view of Green Peter Lake. The pillar offers the potential for high-quality routes with further development.

7. Smack Attack (5.6) ✻✻ Not pictured. This sport climb lies on the bottom half of the rock's south face. Follow three bolts up a ramp then a flake to the belay. This route climbs the Pillar's best rock and is the nicest climb at Highway 11.

8. East Face (5.7 X) Not pictured. This route is very mossy; stay on the cleanest rock possible. The route's bottom half is protected with four bolts. No fixed protection is in place on its top half. This route is not recommended.

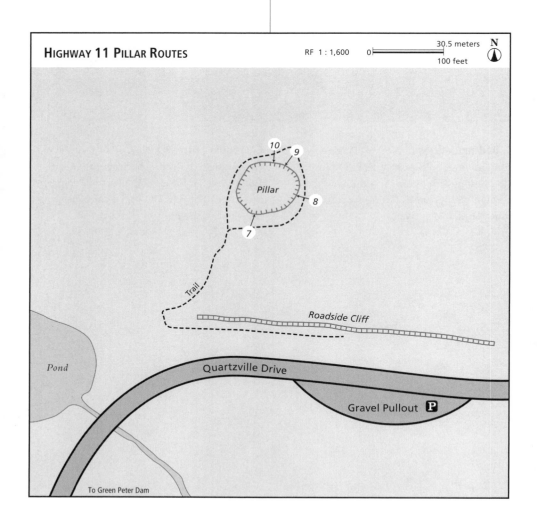

HIGHWAY 11 PILLAR ROUTES   RF 1 : 1,600   0 |—————| 30.5 meters / 100 feet   N

Pillar

Trail

Roadside Cliff

Pond

Quartzville Drive

Gravel Pullout 🅿

To Green Peter Dam

9. Northeast Spine (5.7) ✶ Three bolts lead to a belay on the Pillar's top. This is the shortest and safest route for reaching the summit. The 5.7 crux comes at the route's very top. This exciting crux requires one to surmount a small ceiling to reach the belay. Bad-fall potential exists reaching the first bolt.

10. North Face (5.8) This route is very mossy and slippery. Bad-fall potential exists reaching the first bolt. The rock is steep and has lots of positive edges and pockets. This route lies on the rock's north side. It is dry during summer and early fall months but should be avoided the rest of the year.

LOWER MENAGERIE WILDERNESS

Rock Type	Lava
Quality of Rock (0–5)	4
Maximum Height	200 feet
Ownership	USFS

■ OVERVIEW

The Menagerie Wilderness has several unique lava pillars that lie scattered across a steep and forested ridge. The wilderness's lower portion hosts three main pillars, all of which are well developed. The trails leading to the rocks are maintained. Most of the routes are bolted because this type of rock does not accept traditional protection well. The level of climbing is well suited for beginners and experts, with route grades ranging between 5.5 and 5.11d. The rock is solid and fairly clean. It takes several weeks to climb all of the routes in one's grade. Most of the routes are multiple pitches, and the bolts tend to be spaced far apart. Most routes have 15- to 30-foot runout sections and should be considered R or X rated. Because of the commitment and danger associated with the long runouts, climbers should be very strong

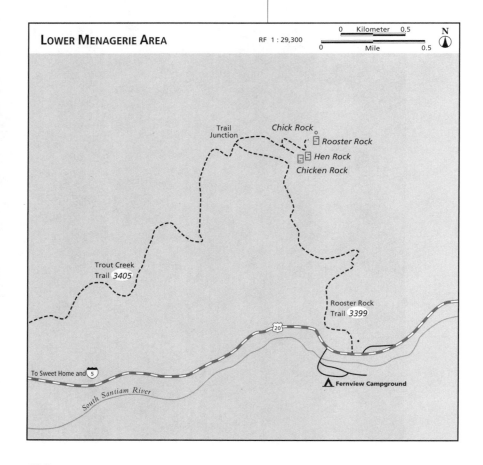

Rooster Rock is a classic climb in the lower Menagerie Wilderness; look for remnants of an old lookout tower near the top.

Adam and Michael testing their skills in the Menagerie Wilderness.

in climbing at least two grade levels above any routes they lead. Fortunately, most pillars have at least one safe and easy climb to their summits. Other routes can be toproped from these positions. Bring sport and traditional gear, and several long runners.

The weather for climbing is best from late spring through fall; winters are wet and there is often snow. The rocks lie at approximately 3,600 feet elevation. The weather changes abruptly in this region of the mountains; take the necessary precautions. Free camping is available off most nearby gravel roads spurring from the highway. Developed campgrounds are found a few miles west on U.S. Highway 20, toward Sweet Home. These campgrounds have facilities such as drinking water and restrooms.

Finding the crags: From the town of Sweet Home, drive east on US 20 for 20 miles. The Rooster Rock Trailhead lies on the highway's north side, just 0.1 mile past Fernview Campground and about 0.5 mile past mile marker 51. Park at the Rooster Rock Trailhead. Follow Rooster Rock Trail 3399 for 1.6 miles to the junction with Trout Creek Trail 3405. Turn right (east) and hike up the hill for 0.3 mile. Continue straight at the first switchback to reach Chicken Rock and Hen Rock, which lie 250 yards down a faint trail. Continue on the main trail through multiple switchbacks for 0.2 mile to reach Rooster Rock. This is a steep and strenuous trail that gains about 2,500 feet elevation over approximately 2.1 miles.

Rooster Rock

Rooster Rock is the largest of the three pillars in the lower Menagerie Wilderness. It used to house an old lookout tower, which can be seen by climbing *Standard Route*. The rock's north face is about 140 feet tall. Given the slope of the mountain, the rock's south face is close to 300 feet tall. The view from the rock's summit is amazing and is well worth the effort required. There are several routes on the rock's southern side that are extremely committing, very runout, and rarely climbed. Consequently, they have not been documented as part of this climbing guide.

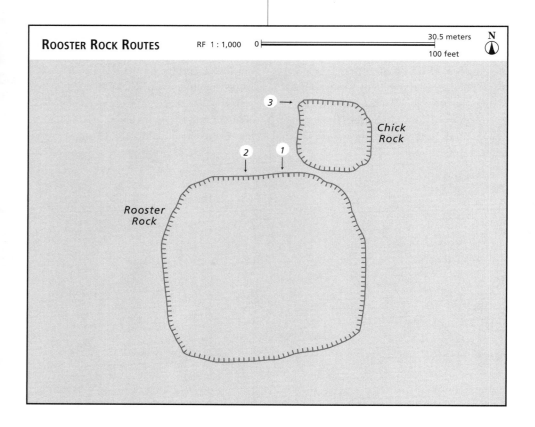

ROOSTER ROCK ROUTES   RF 1 : 1,000   0

30.5 meters
100 feet

N

Chick Rock

Rooster Rock

1. Standard Route (5.6) ★★ This route is easily accomplished in one pitch with a 50-meter rope. It is the easiest and safest route to reach the rock's summit. Climb the ramp to the steep crack between Rooster and Chick Rocks, then climb the crack and face to the notch created by the junction of the two rocks. Climb up and left past several large industrial anchors to the rock's summit. The top portion contains some 5.3 moves but is very runout. To descend, rappel the route in two pitches. Rappel from the summit chains to two large anchors above the steep crack between the two rocks. Reset the rope and rappel from here to the route's base.

2. The Beak (5.10c) ★★
Not pictured. This mixed route sends Rooster Rock's north face and lies 20 feet right of the *Standard Route.* Start on a small dirt ledge just left of a large detached flake. Surmount the flake, then follow several bolts through an overhang up and to the right. This portion of the route is steep but has good holds. Continue up to a steep face, where the route's balancy crux comes toward its top. Climb the face, then surmount a spine-ridge. There are no more bolts from here to the rock's summit; the route's top portion must be protected with traditional gear. Finding solid placements is difficult, which makes this section fairly runout. Climb the spine-ridge up

and left to its top. Continue straight up the broken face, following several discontinuous cracks to the rock's summit. Anchor at the top-belay of the *Standard Route.* To descend, rappel the *Standard Route* in two pitches.

3. Chick's Crack (5.11b) ★ Not pictured. Anchors on Chick Rock's north side allow for toproping the crack-arête on the rock's northwest corner. To set up the toprope, climb the bottom half of the *Standard Route,* then traverse Chick Rock's top ridge to its top anchors. Toprope falls can lead to large swings given the route's overhanging angle. Take the necessary precautions.

Hen Rock

Hen Rock, located downhill 100 yards west-by-southwest from Rooster Rock, has the greatest concentration of good routes. Many of the routes are runout. Gear should be supplemented with a standard rack of traditional gear. **Warning:** The routes on the rock's south and southwest faces are over 90 feet tall; a 60-meter rope barely doubles over to make a toprope. When climbing the routes on the south or southwest faces, belay where the routes meet the *East Slab* route. One-half- to 4-inch traditional gear is needed for setting the belay. To avoid leaving gear, climb *East Slab*'s top portion to the rock's summit and use the top-anchor chains to rappel. Many of the route's first bolts are over 15 feet off the ground. A clip-stick is highly recommended.

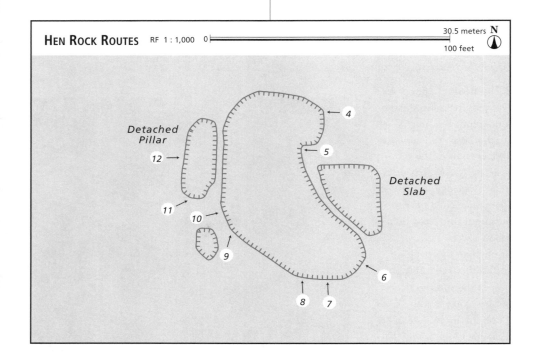

HEN ROCK ROUTES   RF 1 : 1,000   0   30.5 meters N / 100 feet

4. Eggs Overhard (5.11d) ✭✭✭ The powerful crux comes at the route's start. The first bolt is 15 feet off the ground; a clip-stick is recommended. Climb through a series of mini-ramps and vertical sections to a large ceiling. At the last bolt, climb up and left through a slot to the bulge's top. This move is airy and exciting. Move up and left, surmounting the ramp, then climb to the rock's summit and top-chains.

5. East Slab (5.9) ✭✭ Climb the 5.4 crack and ramp to a notch created by a boulder and the rock's south-face ramp. The crack is often covered with vegetation. Step right, then climb the steep ramp to the rock's summit and the top-chains. The route protects well and is the easiest path for reaching the summit. The original published grading on this route was 5.7. Note that a top-belay can be set at the notch halfway up the route. This can be used for toproping the routes on the south and west faces.

6. Southeast Slabs Direct (5.6) ✭ Not pictured. This route follows a crack system on the rock's southeast corner. The crux is mossy; the crack and face make good holds. Climb for 25 feet to a small 5.5 ceiling created by a boulder. Pass the ceiling using the right-side crack to avoid the bushes. Continue up the right-side ramp for 15 feet to a single bolt. Climb a runout ramp up and left for 20 feet and join *Winter Sunshine*. Traditional gear is needed to protect the route and set the top-belay.

7. Winter Sunshine (5.8) ★★ This mixed route climbs the right side of Hen Rock's south face. The steep crux comes at the first bolt. Climb a series of friction holds up the sloping face. Climb past five well-spaced bolts. Step right and climb the easy crack system for 30 feet; bring ½- to 3-inch gear for this section. Continue past two more bolts up a ridge, then a friction slab. This is a tall route, and the top is runout. Bring a standard rack to protect the middle crack system and to set up a top-belay. Cams work best. Belay where the route meets *East Slab.*

8. Summer Rules (5.10b) ★ This route climbs the middle of the south face. The small and balancy crux comes between the first and second bolt. At the ceiling, traverse right then climb over. Move up and left 10 feet to the third bolt. This section is runout, and bad-fall potential exists. Continue up a 5.9 face past one more bolt. Move up and right to a crack system and join *Winter Sunshine* to the top-belay area.

9. Rites of Spring (5.9) ★★ This is an excellent climb, except that the top is extremely runout. It nearly deserves an R rating. The route has an interesting start. Climb the boulder detached from the route's base. Make an exposed step to Hen Rock's southwest face and the route's first bolt. Good holds protect this move, but a fall would be serious. Climb up a steep, friction face with several 5.8+ moves. The good holds are hidden. Halfway up, the route turns easy but very runout. Stay to the ridge's left side, and continue up to the belay area shared with *Winter Sunshine* and *Summer Rules.*

10. Autumn Reigns (5.10b) ★★ This exciting sport route climbs Hen Rock's west face. **Pitch 1:** (5.10b) Start on the right side of the chimney created by the detached pillar. The first bolt is very high; a clip-stick is recommended. The overhanging crux

comes at the second and third bolts. Continue on sloping friction holds to the top-belay at the tree. Bring fresh webbing for the belay. **Pitch 2:** (5.8) From the tree belay, step right to the ramp-face. Climb friction holds past several bolts to the notch on the top of the south face. Use traditional gear to protect the exposed move over the large boulder in the notch. Join the *East Slab* route to the rock's summit and the top-chains.

South Face
Notch Belay

West Face
Tree Belay

11 10 9

12

11. Poached (5.9) ★★ This sport route climbs the rib of the detached pillar's south-west face. The first bolt is 20 feet off the ground; a clip-stick is recommended. **Pitch 1:** (5.9) The crux comes at the first bolt. Climb the staircase rib past several bolts to a solid piton. Climb solid holds on both sides of the arête. At the piton, step right across the chasm to the main pillar, and climb 10 feet to the top-belay at the tree. Bring fresh webbing for the belay. **Pitch 2:** (5.8) Rappel from the tree, or climb the second pitch of *Autumn Reigns* to the rock's summit.

12. Sunnyside Up

(5.10b) ★★ This route sends the detached pillar's west face. The first bolt is 15 feet off the ground, so a clip-stick is highly recommended. **Pitch 1:** (5.9) Start below the wide crack. Follow the steep face past three bolts to a large bushy ledge 10 feet below the detached pillar's top. The crux comes through this first steep section. At the piton, step right across the chasm to the main pillar and climb 10 feet to the top-belay at the tree. Bring fresh webbing for the belay. **Pitch 2:** (5.8) Rappel from the tree, or climb the second pitch of *Autumn Reigns* to the rock's summit.

Chicken Rock

Chicken Rock is located 120 feet downhill from Hen Rock. Chicken Rock's east face is approximately 60 feet tall; its west face is approximately 170 feet tall. It hosts several intimidating and difficult sport routes. Nearly all routes have some significant runout section and should be considered grade R or X. This pillar provides for some fantastic and exciting adventure climbing.

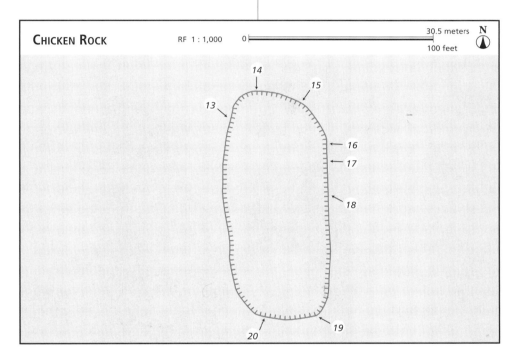

CHICKEN ROCK   RF 1 : 1,000   0

30.5 meters   N

100 feet

14
15
13
16
17
18
19
20

13. Northwest Chimney (5.10d) ★★ This mixed route sends the northwest spine and then the west chimney. Traditional gear is needed to protect the route's middle section through the chimney. Start on the rock's northwest corner next to a fir tree at its base. Climb good holds through several steep bulges for 60 feet. Below a small ceiling next to a bolt, step left. Climb balancy friction holds through the route's technical crux to a ledge. Traverse left at a bush into the west chimney, and climb the brushy but fun chimney to the notch. Turn left and climb the main pillar's runout west face for 30 feet to a bolt. At the last bolt, move right to surmount the overhang, then scramble to the top-chains. Due to its length, this route requires two ropes to rappel, or rappel off the east face.

14. Crystal Ball (5.10d) ★★ The first bolt lies 25 feet off the ground, and the second bolt is 30 feet above the first. Bad ground-fall potential exists. Start 30 feet downhill of the large fir tree and belay area on the northeast corner.

Climb friction holds through a smooth slot, and continue up and right on a fun overhanging face with good holds. Continue up a smooth face to a difficult overhang crux, then continue up the sustained face to the top-chains at the rock's summit. Due to its length, this route requires two ropes to rappel, or rappel off the east face.

15. Chicken Legs (5.11a) ✭✭✭ This is one of the best and most exciting routes in the lower Menagerie Wilderness. Though some bolts are spaced far apart, it is reasonably well protected. Start at the base of the large fir tree on the rock's northeast corner. Climb the ramp past two bolts to a steep overhanging face with several large bulges. The difficult crux comes at the second bulge. Continue up the sustained face through another ceiling to a 5.10c final bulge. Surmounting the final bulge is very airy and intimidating; use a combination of pinches and friction slaps to pull over the top. Scramble 15 feet to the top-chains shared with *Crystal Ball*. Due to its length, this route requires two ropes to rappel, or rappel off the east face.

16. Free Bird
(5.10b) ✭✭ Climb the easy ramp's right side for 30 feet to a steep face; this section is runout. Climb the steep face, through the crux, past three closely spaced bolts to a shallow groove. Scramble up the mossy groove on unprotected rock for 30 feet to a final bolt, then climb the diagonal crack up and left to the top-chains.

17. Sticky Fingers (5.10a) ✭✭ Traverse left on the easy ramp to the first bolt. Climb the ramp past three bolts to the steep east face; the crux comes at the bottom of the face. Climb the face's middle section, following several sparsely spaced bolts, and continue up and left through a shallow groove to the top-chains.

18. Standard Route (5.8) ★★ Climb the ramp past two bolts, then traverse up and left to a notch in the south ridge. Gain the south ridge. Climb good holds on steep rock to the top-chains. Use traditional gear to supplement protection through the route's middle section. This is the easiest route to the pillar's summit.

19. Born of the Forest (5.10b) ★ This route sends Chicken Rock's southeast corner. It is protected with few bolts and should be supplemented with traditional gear. **Pitch 1:** (5.10b) Climb the mossy rock to a steep face, and continue up the face to a bulge. Surmount the bulging crux to the bottom of the east-face ramp. Climb the ramp's

left side for 35 feet to the belay chains. **Pitch 2:** (5.8) Use two ropes to rappel the route, or continue to the rock's summit. From the belay, climb 15 feet to gain the south ridge. Traverse north along the ridge, and join the *Standard Route* to the top-chains.

20. Southern Exposure (5.11c) ✭✭✭ This route's first pitch is very exciting and strenuous. It climbs the rock's steep south face and is a mixed route, as traditional gear is needed to protect most of the bottom pitch. **Pitch 1:** (5.11c) Start downhill on the rock's south side. Climb an unprotected mossy ramp for 25 feet to the first bolt, then climb the overhanging face on superb holds following the placements for natural protection. At the large flat bulge 60 feet up, the route splits and has a left and right variation. *Left Variation:* At the bulge's bottom, traverse left and climb a shallow groove passing two bolts to a steep overhanging dihedral. Climb the sustained overhanging 5.11c dihedral past three closely spaced bolts. Surmount the small ceiling and gain the east ramp, then climb the ramp 10 feet to the belay chains. *Right Variation (south face):* At the bulge's bottom, move up and right to a shallow overhanging groove with parallel cracks. Climb the strenuous overhanging cracks to a steep bulge.

Power through the 5.11a overhanging crux to gain the east-side ramp, then climb the ramp 15 feet to the belay chains. **Pitch 2:** (5.8) Use two ropes to rappel the route, or continue to the rock's summit. From the belay, climb 15 feet to gain the south ridge. Traverse north along the ridge, and join the *Standard Route* to the top-chains.

SHARK FIN ROCK

Rock Type	Volcanic
Quality of Rock (0–5)	3
Maximum Height	35 feet
Ownership	USFS

■ OVERVIEW

Shark Fin Rock is a fin-shaped pinnacle that lies in a clear-cut east of the Menagerie Wilderness. It has one sport route and one short toprope. The lava rock provides lots of friction and good holds. Some sections are mossy, but the *East Face* sport route is relatively clean. It takes a few hours to hike to the rock, climb both routes, and hike back to the parking area. The road is often blocked with snow and debris throughout the winter, but the rest of the year the rock is accessible for climbing. This area offers beautiful views of the surrounding mountains, and there are many places to explore in the vicinity. Free camping is available throughout the area, but drinking water and restrooms are not.

This section of mountains contains many pillars and pinnacles, but few have been climbed. Most of the rock is mossy and makes poor climbing until

cleaned. Still, the area can provide lots of first ascents.

Finding the crags: Follow U.S. Highway 20 east from Sweet Home. Drive 21 miles and turn north onto Soda Fork Road (USFS Road 2041), which lies 0.5 mile east of mile marker 52 and just before Mountain House. Follow Soda Fork Road for 1.8 miles and turn left (west) onto a narrow, brushy, gravel road. This brush can scratch a vehicle; take the necessary precautions. Go 1.1 miles and turn left (south) on another gravel road. Follow this road 0.25 mile, and park on the landing at the top of the hill.

No man-made trails lead to the pillar, so easy bushwhacking is required. Start to the east of the small cliff on the landing, and hike due north for 150 yards. The pillar lies in the clear-cut 30 yards east of the ridgetop. Stay near the top but to the ridge's east side.

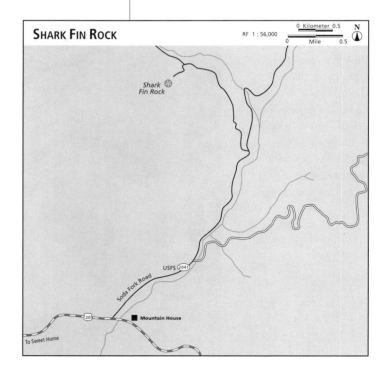

Shark Fin Rock is a fin-shaped pinnacle with some nice views of the Cascades.

Shark Fin Rock

The top-belay consists of two bolts on top of the rock's west side.

1. East Face (5.9 R) ✹✹ Start on the pillar's downhill side. The 5.9 crux is protected well with three bolts. The holds are solid and clean, but hidden. Afterwards, the route is unprotected. Climb the easy spine to the belay on the rock's west side. The runout exposure intimidates many climbers.

2. Southwest Corner (5.5) Not pictured. After reaching the summit, it is possible to toprope the pillar's southwest face. Navigate the easy ramp, then traverse left to the top anchors. The route is 20 feet tall.

WOLF ROCK

Rock Type	Volcanic
Quality of Rock (0–5)	4
Maximum Height	1,000 feet
Ownership	USFS

■ OVERVIEW

Wolf Rock has several great sport routes. Climbing is well suited for beginners and experts, with routes ranging from 5.1 to 5.13. Climbing all of the routes in one's grade would take several days. The rock is well developed with bolts and top anchors in place. This type of rock does not accept traditional protection very well. The trails leading to the rock can be hard to find. Snow blocks access to the rock during the winter and early spring, but the rest of the year offers good climbing. The rock is solid and fairly clean, though sand and moss cover some of the uncleaned portions. The multitude of horizontal edges makes for great climbing. Some of the bolts are spaced far apart, and the older bolts are getting weak. Take the necessary precautions. One can camp anywhere in the area, but drinking water and restrooms are not available.

Finding the crags: Follow U.S. Highway 20 east from Sweet Home for 30 miles. Turn south onto Deer Creek Road (USFS Road 15), which is approximately 1 mile after Civil Road. Follow Deer Creek Road for 12 miles to Wolf Rock. Road signs are periodically in place. Or, follow Highway 126 east from Eugene to Blue River Reservoir. Turn north onto Blue River Road (USFS Road 15) and follow it for 14.5 miles to Wolf Rock. A few small pullouts in the vicinity make good parking areas.

The Amphitheater

The Amphitheater lies 200 yards southwest of the Great Arch and is an interesting natural feature. It provides great scrambling. The easiest route to the summit of Wolf Rock, and the most common descent route, lies just over the ridge west of the Amphitheater. Two approaches lead to the bottom of the route. Hike up the creek bed to the Amphitheater, then go west over the small ridge to the next gully. Or, start 150 feet west of the creek in the timber. Hike straight up the hill to the gully, which contains the start of the route.

1. SW Scramble / Descent Route (5.1) ★★
Not pictured. The round-trip to the summit and back takes most of a day and is characteristic of a mountaineering route. Steep scrambling with intense exposure leads all of the way to the summit. There are no bolts on the route. Bring a few nuts, several slings, a rope, and watch out for loose rock. **Pitch 1:** (5.1) Scramble up the creek bed in the gully west of the Amphitheater, and stop 25 feet below the vertical wall in the gully. Traverse up and left to the top of the ridge between the two gullies. From here, climb up 30 feet to the top of the wall. This section may be more than one pitch depending upon where you start climbing. To descend this section, downclimb or rappel. If you rappel, you will have to leave gear. There are no bolts on the route. **Pitch 2–5:** (4th class) Easy scrambling brings you to the summit ridge. Stay in the gully as long as you wish; eventually it is easier scrambling up the ridge to the east (right). Follow this ridge for several hundred feet to where it opens up and flattens out. From here, take your desired path to the summit ridge. **Summit Ridge:** (3rd class) Once on the summit ridge, follow it northeast to the true summit. A summit registry is available to document your climb. One of

WOLF ROCK

RF 1 : 392,000

Kilometers

Miles

N

To Sweet Home

20

Deer Creek Road

(USFS 15)

Wolf
Rock

Blue River

Blue River Road

(USFS 15)

Blue River Lake

126

To Eugene

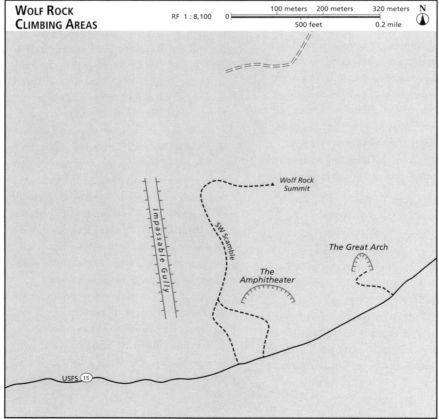

WOLF ROCK
CLIMBING AREAS

RF 1 : 8,100

100 meters 200 meters 320 meters

500 feet 0.2 mile

N

Impassable Gully

Wolf Rock
Summit

SW Scramble

The Great Arch

The
Amphitheater

USFS 15

At 1,000 feet tall, the massive monolith Wolf Rock has the potential to be a climbing mecca.

The Great Arch—Southeast Wall

the books dates back to 1964, and it provides interesting reading. To descend, backtrack the route. Be careful. The climb takes about six to eight hours round-trip.

The Great Arch —Southeast Wall

The best sport climbing is found on the Southeast Wall. Hike up the small talus field to the large arch-shaped ceiling in the east face. Start adjacent to the right-side timberline. In 100 feet the brush clears. Hike through the middle of the talus field. Toward the top, before the trees, a faint trail leads up and left. Follow it 50 feet, then switchback up and right to the wall's base. Hike along the rock's base for 50 feet to reach the routes.

2. Spine Buster (5.8) ✷✷✷ This excellent sport route climbs the spine's lower portion to the ceiling's north side. The crux comes right below the second bolt. The rest of the route has good holds, and the bolts are spaced closely.

3. Spine Sender (5.10d R) ✷✷ This route

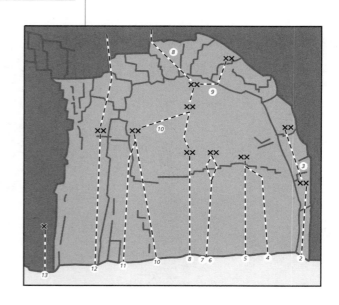

lies above *Spine Buster*. It climbs the over-hanging portion of the spine and ends near the top of the large ceiling. The route's bottom portion is very runout. The distance from the belay on top of *Spine Buster* to the first bolt is nearly 25 feet; this section grades 5.10a. Use small pieces of protection to reduce the possibility of a bad fall. The bolt spacing is good from the first bolt to the top. The technical crux comes between the third and fourth bolts. The end of the route is very exciting. A large overhang must be climbed to reach the top-belay; this section has great holds. Watch out for loose rock at the route's beginning and end.

4. Unchained (5.10d)
★★ Once this route is finished being bolted, it will be a great one. Currently, it makes a terrific toprope. Leading the route can be done

but is not recommended. It is runout traversing from the last bolt, up to the last bolt of *Cold Shut*. The route weaves its way up small edges on steep rock. There are few good resting holds, so it tests your endurance.

5. Cold Shut (5.9) ✯✯✯ This sport route is an area classic. It is tall and vertical and ascends a black watermark. The technical crux lies in the middle of the route. Tackling the small ceiling toward the top of the watermark is a test of endurance. Sometimes the route can be wet in spots. There are great holds throughout, though some of them are hidden.

6. Forked Route (5.10c) ✯✯✯ This steep route shares the start with *CrackerJacks*. At the small ceiling halfway up, it leads to the right. The crux comes just above the second-to-the-last bolt, and requires making moves on little edges with poor footholds.

7. CrackerJacks (5.11a) ✯✯✯ This sport climb splits left from *Forked Route* at the ceiling halfway up. The crux comes while climbing through the small overhang. The route's difficulty is fairly sustained from this point on.

8. Stairs to the Stars (5.10d) ✯✯✯ Pitch 1 is an excellent sport route. It is recommended to stop here instead of wrecking the experience with pitches 2 and 3. **Pitch 1:** (5.10d) Supersteep rock combined with fluid moves makes this a classic. The holds are great. The

technical crux comes right above the ceiling. Some of the bolts are spaced far apart. **Pitch 2:** (5.9 R) One bolt protects this 25-foot pitch. The climbing is nothing special and very runout. The crux comes just above the belay, before the first bolt. After that, the route drops off to 5.5. **Pitch 3:** (5.7) This is a really short pitch. Though it does lead to the wall's

top, which provides a great view, the climbing is rather dull. The rock and bolt spacings are good, and the holds are large and blocky. The rappel is tall and fun. It requires two 50-meter ropes, which barely reach the ground.

9. Shanghai (5.13a, C2) ★★ This route is extremely difficult. It ascends the huge over-hanging ceiling at the arch's top, and is so overhanging that climbers have a difficult time aid-climbing it. The bolts are closely spaced. Several carabiners and some aiders are all that is required to aid-climb it. The top-belay is set in an awkward position. A double-rope rappel with two 60-meter ropes gets one down from the ceiling's top.

10. Brand X (5.8) ★★ This tall pitch follows the large black watermark on the south side of the great ceiling. Some of the bolts lie far apart. Large ledges and holds make it fairly easy.

11. Solstice Party (5.10b) ★★ This good, clean route shares anchors with *Brand X*. It ascends a steep section of the wall covered with good holds. The flat crux comes around the third bolt. Making the fourth clip is awk-ward and difficult. A 60-meter rope is required.

12. Get Up Stand Up (5.10b) ★★★ Wander up the good rock on solid holds. The last bolt is runout, but the holds are good. The technical crux comes just above the route's midpoint. Footholds disappear through a long lock-off. This relatively new route requires a 60-meter rope.

13. Project (5.6 R) This route is mostly avoided. It winds its way up huge, mossy ledges for three bolts. Getting to the first bolts is easy, but very runout. Beware, there is no belay at the top; there is only some web-bing strung through a single bolt. Bring web-bing to rappel off. Climbing this poor route is not recommended.

SANTIAM PINNACLE

Rock Type	Volcanic
Quality of Rock (0–5)	3
Maximum Height	200 feet
Ownership	USFS

■ OVERVIEW

Santiam Pinnacle provides sport climbing and toproping. Several old, runout routes have recently been retro-bolted. They protect well and provide fun, relaxed climbing. The area is still being developed. The level of climbing ranges from beginner to intermediate, and routes grade between 5.1 and 5.11c. It takes two days to climb all of the routes. Snow covers the area during winter; climbing is best spring through fall. Much of the uncleaned rock is mossy. The lower rock is flaky and less solid; the higher rock is solid and sticky. Rockfall is common. The area lies above 3,000 feet, where thunderstorms and other weather patterns can develop quickly. Take the necessary precautions. Most approaches require semitechnical, exposed scrambling. Timid hikers may want to avoid this area. Free camping is available off any of the nearby roads stemming from U.S. Highway 20. Drinking water and restrooms are unavailable. Pay-camping sites can be found along US 20, toward Sweet Home.

Finding the crags: Follow US 20 east from Sweet Home for 29 miles. The pinnacle lies on the north side of the highway, 0.5 mile after mile marker 60. A large pullout on the south side of the highway provides good parking. The area descriptions below contain directions to reach each rock.

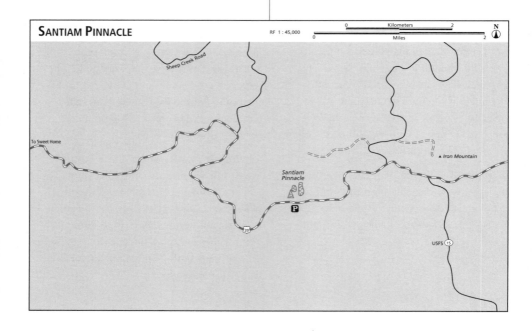

Santiam Pinnacle lies right off the highway and provides climbing for both beginners and experts.

Santiam Pinnacle

To reach the pinnacle, hike up the talus slope below the rocks. Continue for 300 feet until a wall is reached, turn right and follow the wall. Ascend a dirt ramp between the wall and a dead stump. At the pinnacle's base, hike downhill for 30 feet to reach the South Face. To access the upper routes, hike uphill along the pinnacle's base. Continue for 25 feet until a wall blocks the approach, then traverse left across a dirt gully. Scramble up 10 feet and follow an exposed rock-ramp up and right

toward the pinnacle. Scramble another 20 feet to the pinnacle's base. A small cave makes a good staging area.

1. South Face (5.4)★★★ Not pictured. This is a fun and well-protected route that's great for beginners. The third pitch is not bolted. The summit view is spectacular, and the exposure is thrilling. The *South Face* is an area classic. **Pitch 1:** (5.4) A chimney splits the middle of the south face. Start on the chimney's left side and continue past several bolts to a ridge. Climb the easy ridge to a small vertical wall, and ascend the wall's left side to

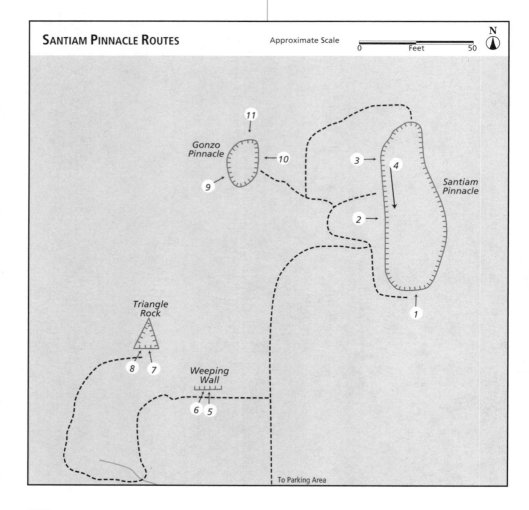

SANTIAM PINNACLE ROUTES   Approximate Scale   0   Feet   50   N

the belay. **Pitch 2:** (5.4) Climb the left-side ridge for 25 feet. Traverse up and right to a broken dihedral system, and climb up 20 feet. The wall's steepness forces an exposed step left. Continue past several more bolts to a belay in a chimney. **Pitch 3:** (5.3) This pitch is not bolted and is runout. A medium-size cam can be used to reduce exposure. Climb up the south-face ramp to a break in the summit, then climb through to a belay at the top. Top anchors are in place for rappelling.

2. Water Buffalo (5.11c) ✶✶ This unfinished sport route tackles a difficult roof on the pinnacle's west face. The roof's rock is sharp. The pumpy crux requires a knee-bar and a long lock-off. Currently, the route can only be toproped; top anchors are in place. To set up a toprope, climb the *South Face* to the pinnacle's top and rappel down to *Water Buffalo*'s top anchors.

3. The Boz (5.10a) ✭ This is a single-pitch toprope, with the steep crux coming at the route's top. There are no bolts in place. Traditional gear is needed for setting up a toprope. Reduce rope drag by using long runners to set the rope over the rock's edge. To set up a toprope, scramble up the gully between Santiam and Gonzo Pinnacles. At the top, hike right for 30 feet to Santiam Pinnacle's north face and scramble 20 feet to the north summit's base.

4. The Crawl (5.1 R) ✭ This route traverses a small ledge across the pinnacle's west face. There are no bolts, and traditional protection is nearly nonexistent. The exposure and awkward moves, however, are thrilling. Start at the belay area at the top of *The Boz*. Traverse the small ledge for 25 feet, then downclimb a few feet and cross a small gully to the belay anchors. From here, it is possible to scramble down to the top of the *South Face*'s second pitch.

Weeping Wall

To reach the wall, hike up the talus slope below the rocks. Continue for 100 feet until the trail narrows between a rock wall on the left and a fir tree on the right. Weeping Wall lies 30 feet to the left.

5. Weeping Wall (5.10b) ✶✶✶ Not pictured. This short route climbs three bolts to the top anchors. It is steep, fun, and pumpy. The bulging crux comes above the third bolt. This tricky crux has sent multiple climbers into the air.

6. Nuts n Bolts (A1) ✶ Not pictured. A short bolt-ladder rises 10 feet to the left of *Weeping Wall*. Aid-climb straight up, then traverse right to *Weeping Wall*'s top anchors. Use small nuts to place over the bolts; most of them do not have hangers. This dull aid-line is not highly recommended, but it provides good practice for beginning aid-climbers.

Triangle Rock

To reach Triangle Rock, continue past Weeping Wall. No man-made trails lead to the rock. Hike along the wall for 40 feet and cross a very small creek bed. Ascend a dirt ramp for 30 feet, then traverse the dirt ramp right for 30 feet to the belay area. This section of the approach is difficult and exposed. Extreme caution is recommended.

7. Batman (5.7) ✶✶ This route sends the right-side face of Triangle Rock. *Batman* and *Triangular Bush* share top anchors. Most of the route grades 5.5. The deceiving crux lies at the third bolt.

8. Triangular Bush (5.7) ✶✶✶ This route is an area classic. Start directly below the first bolt, using caution to get to the first clip. The balancy crux sends a series of small edges, and lies between the third and fifth bolts. This part of the route is protected very well. Clipping the top anchors is slightly awkward.

Gonzo Pinnacle

To reach the routes, hike to Santiam Pinnacle's upper staging area. Scramble up the right side of the gully between Gonzo and Santiam Pinnacles. Cross the gully 10 feet below the large fir tree to reach the rock's base.

9. Go Gonzo (5.5) Not pictured. This runout route climbs the pinnacle's west side. The rock is mossy and loose. No bolts are in place except for the top-belay; traditional gear is needed. Avoiding this route is strongly recommended.

10. Archimedes

(5.7) ★★ This short four-bolt sport route climbs the pinnacle's east face. Start on the rock's upper, east side. Follow three bolts through a small overhang, then climb a 5.1 ramp for 20 feet to the top anchors.

11. Solo Superstar (5.1, A1, 5.4) ★ This short route is the easiest way to gain the pinnacle's summit. Start in the saddle on the pinnacle's north side, and make a 5.4 move to gain a large ledge on the rock's east side. Step left and clip the route's single, good bolt. At this point, the route joins *Archimedes*. Climb a 5.1 ramp for 20 feet to the top anchors. The route's bottom 15 feet sends a bolted ladder and can be aid-climbed. Use small nuts to place over the bolts; they do not have hangers.

IRON WALL

Rock Type	Volcanic
Quality of Rock (0–5)	2
Maximum Height	90 feet
Ownership	Private

■ OVERVIEW

The rock at Iron Wall does not accept protection; the area provides bouldering and topropes. The level of climbing ranges from beginner to intermediate, with most routes grading 5.8 and below (there is one 5.12). All routes can be climbed in a day. The area is relatively undeveloped. There are no man-made trails leading to the wall, but the rock lies in a clear-cut, so they are unnecessary. The climbing season runs from late spring through fall. Snow blocks access to the area during the winter. The rock is good on the cleaned routes, but the uncleaned rock is covered with moss and loose holds. Few routes are thoroughly cleaned. Much of the rock is steep and covered with pea-size to softball-size nubbins. This provides a different experience for most climbers. Lots of debris tends to fall off the cliff; take the necessary precautions. All routes have top anchors in place, and many are set over the cliff's edge. Caution is necessary when searching for the anchors and setting up topropes. One can camp anywhere in the area, but drinking water and restrooms are unavailable.

Finding the crags: From the town of Sweet Home, follow U.S. Highway 20 east for 31 miles. A quarter mile after mile marker 62, turn north onto Civil Road. Follow Civil Road for 1 mile, then turn north onto USFS Road 038. Follow USFS 038 for 1.5 miles to a large junction and turn right onto an unnamed road. The rock is visible from this point. Follow the road for 30 feet, then turn left onto another unnamed road. Follow this road 100 feet and park. Hike to the hill's top, east side. Look closely and carefully over the edge for toprope anchors. Hike around the rock's east side to get to the bottom of the routes.

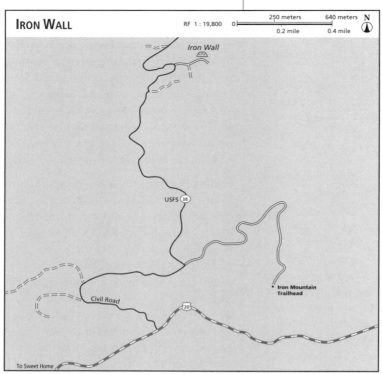

IRON WALL

RF 1 : 19,800

250 meters · 640 meters · N

0.2 mile · 0.4 mile

Iron Wall

USFS 38

Civil Road

20

Iron Mountain
Trailhead

To Sweet Home

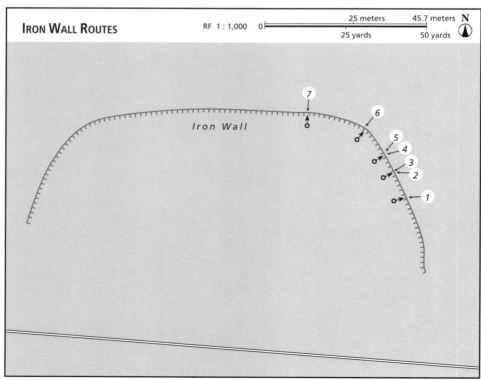

IRON WALL ROUTES

RF 1 : 1,000

25 meters · 45.7 meters · N

25 yards · 50 yards

Iron Wall

7

6

5

4

3

2

1

Iron Wall is nestled in the hills of the Cascade Range, with lots of room for development.

Iron Wall

Iron Wall is on private property, owned by a timber company. Access is currently permitted but may be closed off at any time. Watch for signs restricting access. Toprope anchors are in place for every climb. Long runners are sometimes necessary to reduce rope drag.

1. Pristine Christine (5.4) ★ This route lies farthest to the south. Climb the huge holds up the angled face. The top is the steepest, but is still very easy.

2. Iron Gland (5.5) ✦ This is a variation to the start of *Bold Beef Brain*. Start directly below the anchors and climb straight up. The crux comes at the bottom, and the rest of the route is relatively easy.

3. Bold Beef Brain (5.7) ✦ The crux comes at the start of the route and requires one tricky move. The route has huge nubbins, and some sections are mossy.

4. Space Case (5.7) ✶ Start to the right of the gully, and climb up to the left side of the cave. The crux is a large step as you pull over the left side of the cave.

5. Atomic Ephrum (5.8) ✶ Start 8 feet to the right of *Space Case*. This is a steep route that climbs over the right side of the cave. The crux comes as you climb on small nubbins passing the cave.

6

6. Dover the Arête (5.8) ★★ This is one of the cleanest routes on the wall and an area classic. Climb straight up the arête. The crux requires balanced climbing on spaced-out nubbins through a vertical section in the wall.

7. TNT (5.12c) ✶ The bottom of this route is great, but the top is mossy and degrades it to one star. It is recommended to stop halfway up. The crux comes as you leave the over-hang at the bottom of the route. This section takes lots of strength and balance. During develop-ment, the grade increased when a flake hold pulled off the overhang's roof.

GREEN RIDGE

Rock Type	Basalt
Quality of Rock (0–5)	2
Maximum Height	45 feet
Ownership	USFS

■ OVERVIEW

The climbing area is a cliff band sitting on the east side of Green Ridge. It has several toprope routes. There are no bolts on the cliff. The level of climbing ranges from beginner to intermediate; routes range from 5.6 to 5.11a. The rock is mostly solid with some loose and dirty sections. The area provides a couple days of climbing, which is best in spring and fall due to snow in the winter and extreme heat during the summer. Rockfall is common, so take the necessary precautions. Also be prepared for the arid climate. One can camp anywhere in the area. Services such as drinking water and restrooms are not available.

Finding the crags: From the town of Sisters, drive west on U.S. Highway 20 for 6 miles. Just after mile marker 95, turn north onto USFS Road 11 (Green Ridge Road). There are many side roads, so make sure you stay on the correct road. Follow USFS 11 for 15.7 miles. The cliff is 30 feet up the hill on the left. A few pullouts in the vicinity make good parking areas. Scramble up the dirt hill in one of the more obviously easy places.

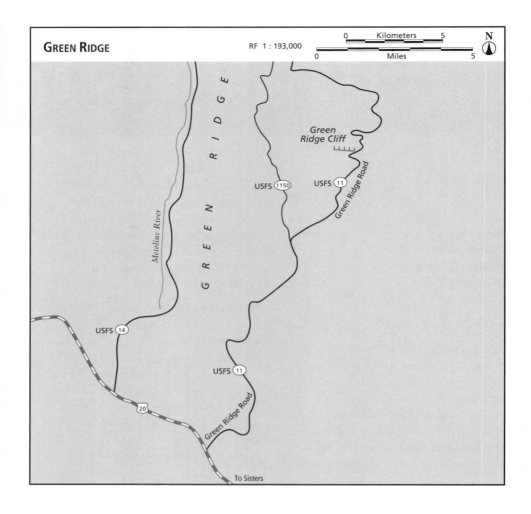

GREEN RIDGE

RF 1 : 193,000

Kilometers 0 — 5

Miles 0 — 5

N

GREEN RIDGE

Green Ridge Cliff

Metolius River

USFS 1150   USFS 11

Green Ridge Road

USFS 14

USFS 11

Green Ridge Road

20

To Sisters

This arid climbing area is located on the east side of Green Ridge.

Green Ridge

1. Avoidance (5.6) ✴ Scramble up the large block then dirt ramp to the small overhanging dihedral section. Stem through then traverse left, on the ramp, to the crack in the corner. Climb up a few feet, then traverse up and right, across the ramp, to the crack on the right side of the face. From here to the top is the best section of the route. It is a little difficult to find good protection for setting up a toprope.

2. Pine Soda (5.8) ★ This route starts well, but awkward moves and dirty rock degrade it significantly. Climb the face, between the crack and the arête, to the top. The toprope is difficult to set up, but there is plenty of hidden good protection.

3. Webster (5.11a) ★★ This is the best route on the cliff. Start on the crescent-shaped ramp, and climb up to the small overhang. Move right to the crack, up a few feet, then back left onto the face. The whole top is slightly overhanging and requires crimping and edging on tiny ledges. There are good holds, however. Watch for loose rock on top when setting up a toprope.

4. Makeup (5.9) ★★ This route appears to be 5.11, but the good holds make it much easier. The rock is fairly solid and clean the whole way. Start on the right side of the face, and climb up to the big ledges halfway.

Step left and climb the arête and face to the top. The crux comes at the flat section above the halfway ledge. The top is a little loose, so be careful. Finding good protection for topropes can be difficult. A large supply of long runners is recommended.

5. Champ (5.10a) ★ Climb the crack that splits the face sticking out toward the road. The bottom is covered with loose rock; the top provides good protection for setting up topropes. The crux comes at the bottom of the crack where the flat face bulges. Knee bars, arm bars, jams, and liebacks may all be necessary.

SISTERS
BOULDERS

Rock Type	Volcanic
Quality of Rock (0–5)	4
Maximum Height	30 feet
Ownership	USFS

■ OVERVIEW

The Sisters Boulders provide bouldering and
topropes. The rock is difficult to protect with
traditional gear. The level of climbing ranges
from beginner to expert, with many routes
grading harder than 5.10. It takes a week to
climb all of the routes in one's grade. The
area is well developed, and has good trails

and a sectioned-off parking area. Many
toprope anchors are in place. Climbing year-
round is possible, but winters are cold and
there may be snow. The sticky rock creates
superb holds that allow for gymnastic moves
through large overhangs. The rock is also
very sharp and sometimes flaky; some
climbers protect their fingers with tape.
Some routes still have loose holds, so it is
recommended to check the holds before
pulling on them. Verify the descents before
committing to a problem. One can camp
anywhere in the area, but drinking water and
restrooms are unavailable.

Most of the boulder problems can be
easily found by using the overview maps.
When a topo is used, "see topo" appears in
the route description.

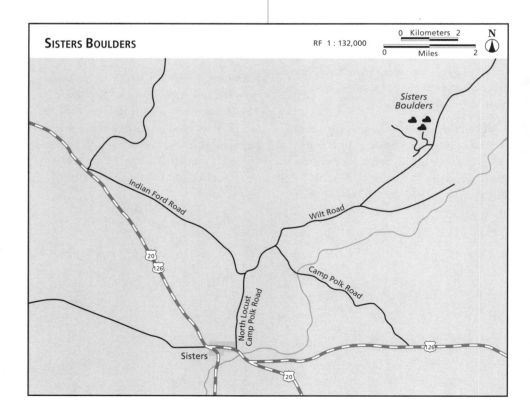

This volcanic playground provides boulders aplenty.

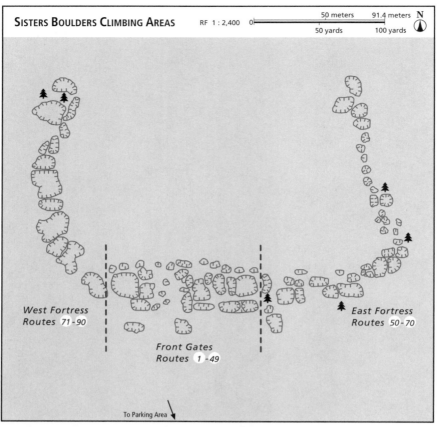

50 meters   91.4 meters   N

50 yards   100 yards

West Fortress
Routes 71 - 90

East Fortress
Routes 50 - 70

Front Gates
Routes 1 - 49

To Parking Area

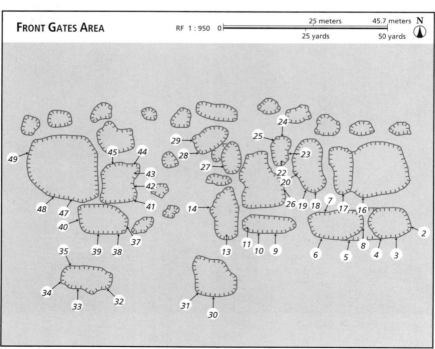

FRONT GATES AREA   RF 1 : 950   0

25 meters   45.7 meters   N

25 yards   50 yards

Adam bouldering at Sisters Boulders.

Finding the crags: From the east side of Sisters on U.S. Highway 20, turn north onto North Locust Road, which turns into Camp Polk Road after 2 blocks. Follow Camp Polk Road until it turns into Wilt Road, and continue along Wilt Road until it turns to gravel. From this point, drive 2.5 miles. After mile marker 5, turn west onto an unnamed dirt road. A tree with a white P and two red reflectors marks the turnoff. Drive 200 yards and turn right onto the first dirt road. Follow this road another 200 yards to the parking area.

Front Gates

1. Big Daddy (5.10a) ✶✶✶ Start on *Smack Daddy*. Traverse both rocks the whole way around, from *Smack Daddy* to Route 6. This route tests one's endurance. The crux comes at a bulge on the north side of the east rock.

2. Smack Daddy (5.10a) ✶✶ Climb the great jugs, which lead to thinner holds through the bulging crux.

3. Zorro (5.7) ✶✶✶ This route is a classic. Use the positive holds to follow the broken seam.

4. Big Brother (5.7) ✶ The top is awkward, but most climbers still enjoy the route.

5. Grass Stain (5.11a) ✶ See topo. Fun pockets lead to a painful crack that breaks the ceiling.

6. Unknown (5.8) ✶ See topo. Follow the overhanging crack through the ceiling.

7. Unknown (5.6) ✶ This climb has bad-fall potential and is not recommended.

8. Unknown (5.3) ✶✶ See topo. Climb the chimney between the two rocks. Jam the west-side crack as needed. This is the easiest route to the top of the rocks.

9. Hammer Time (5.9) ✶✶ See topo. The bulging crux comes midway. From there, fun jugs lead to the top.

10. Blankman (5.8) ✶✶ See topo. Climb straight up the rock's middle. The huge jug, midway, is helpful.

11. A55 (5.8) ✶ See topo. Climb the face, following the broken seam. Some moves at midway are awkward.

12. Crumblecake (5.9) ✶✶ Start on the rock's east side, and traverse the south face. This is a pleasant route with solid rock, despite the name.

13. Alez (5.10b) ✶✶✶ See topo. Follow good holds to the huge south-side overhang, and tackle it head on. Great holds take one to the top.

14. Sasquatch (5.7) See topo. Climb the mossy, awkward crack on the rock's west side. The crack protects with cams. This is the best route for gaining the summit to set up topropes for Routes 9 through 13.

15. Lunar Gravity (5.10a) ✶✶✶ See topo. This is a classic traverse, with an extreme overhang that tests one's strength. Start on the rock's east side and traverse the south face.

16. Unknown (5.9) ✶ The start to this route is tricky and entertaining. The rock is mossy near the top.

17. Unknown (5.8) ✶✶ Climb the fun nubbins to the rock's top.

18. Unknown (5.7) ✶✶ Climb the exciting bulge near the top.

19. Unknown (5.8) ✶✶ This entire route offers fluid moves and good edges.

20. Unknown (5.7) ✶✶ Climb a few feet, then tackle the exciting friction slaps near the top.

21. Unknown (5.9) ✶✶ Start at Route 18, and traverse the rock's west face. The crux comes toward the end.

22. Unknown (5.6) ✶ This route follows good rock, but is very short.

23. Unknown (5.3) ✶ This easy climb makes a good warm-up. Use it to descend the rock.

24. Unknown (5.10a) ✶ This flat wall only has two difficult moves.

25. Unknown (5.7) ✶✶ Climb the fun arête. This route is short.

26. Unknown (5.7) ✶ Climb the powerful overhang to complete this route.

27. Unknown (5.11b) ✶ This problem takes a lot of power. Beware of mossy rock.

28. Unknown (5.5) ✶✶ This climb offers fun moves on solid jugs.

29. Unknown (5.5) ✶ Secure, easy moves make this a good beginner route. It is very short.

30. Unknown (5.7) ✶✶✶ Use long reaches to move between great holds. This airy face is enjoyed by most climbers.

31. Unknown (5.8) ✶ Use power to gain the start. This route is very short.

32. Unknown (5.7) ✶ Lieback and climb the crack. This mediocre route is not highly recommended.

33. Unknown (5.11c) ✶✶✶ Strong fingers and superb balance are needed to defeat this bulging crux.

34. Unknown (5.8) ✶✶✶ This route is bulgy at the start with an exciting, airy crux.

35. Unknown (5.4) Use this route to descend the rock. It is difficult to see the footholds while downclimbing; a partner can be helpful.

36. Unknown (5.10c) ✶✶ Start below *Poison,* and traverse the overhanging south face. Most climbers stop at the tree.

37. Poison (5.11c) ✶✶✶ Start on the pillar's east side next to the small boulder, and climb mediocre holds to the overhang. Dyno off a small pinch to a great hold, or use a hidden undercling to surpass the small pinch.

38. 3 Things (5.10d) ★★★ The crux requires a long lock-off three-quarters of the way up.

39. BW (5.10a) ★★★ Climb the powerful jugs to a knob. The difficulty eases beyond this point.

40. Unknown (5.3) ★★ This easy, tall route is enjoyable. Use it to gain the top for setting up topropes.

41. Unknown (5.9) ★ This route has bad-fall potential and is not highly recommended.

42. Unknown (5.9) ★★ Use good jugs to power through the bulge.

43. Can't You Do It Crux Wuss? (5.10a) ★★★ Climb up and over the outside bulge.

44. Unknown (5.11d) ★ This powerful crux requires using a one-finger pocket. The route has bad-fall potential. The flake moves when weighted; use caution.

45. Unknown (5.9) ★ This route offers good pockets, but it is not recommended because of bad-fall potential.

46. Unknown (5.2) This short climb is the easiest way to reach the top of the rock. Use it as a descent route for Routes 41 through 45.

47. Blue Moon (5.8) ★ Climb the center of the rock's first good bulge. This route is not highly recommended.

48. Capital Offense (5.8) ★★ Climb the good jugs to the rock's top. A large stack of pine needles sits on top; use caution.

49. Starstruck (5.10c) ★ Climb up the face's middle. The middle bulge is challenging.

East Fortress

50. Unknown (5.10c) ★ Climb the small edges to the rock's top. A close tree interferes with one's climbing.

51. Unknown (5.11b) ★★ Climb tiny edges up the overhanging east face.

52. Unknown (5.5) ★★★ Use the great nubbins to climb this rampy face.

53. Unknown (5.5) ★ One long reach between good holds completes this route.

54. Unknown (5.9) ★ Climb the broken face through two bulges.

55. Unknown (5.11c) ★★ Traverse the rock's south face. Finishing the west bulge makes this route much more difficult.

56. Point of Grace (5.8) ★★★ Use long reaches between good holds to climb the rock's face.

57. Snarfalarfagus (5.8) ★★ Climb on good holds through the broken overhang.

58. Unknown (5.11c) ★★ This route's lower bulge is difficult, but the difficulty eases midway up.

59. Unknown (5.8 to 5.10c) ★ Traverse the rock's southeast face. The grade depends on the height at which one traverses the route.

60. Deep Well (5.10d) ★★★ Climb the middle of the rock's face, following the seam. There is no easy way down from the rock's top.

61. Unknown (5.8) ★★ Climb the outside overhang. This route has great nubbins.

62. Unknown (5.10a) ★★★ Climb the blank, overhanging face. The moves are short but fluid.

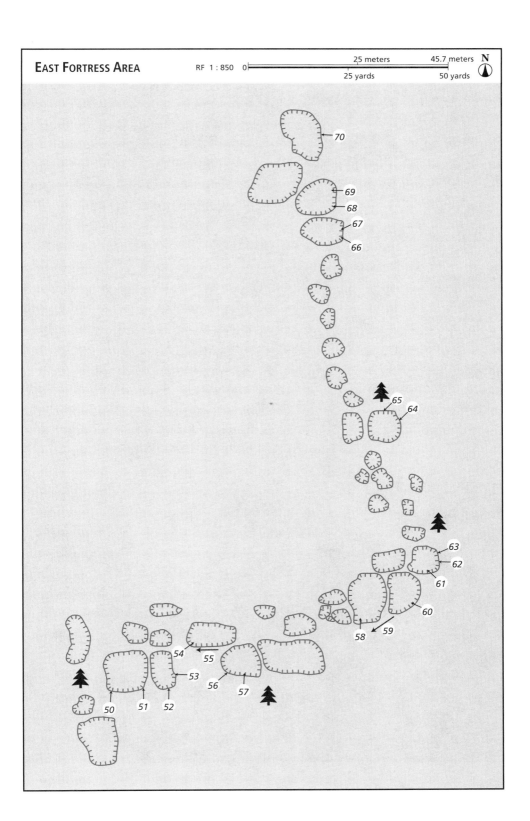

63. Unknown (5.8) ✶ Climb the knobby east face.

64. Unknown (5.7) ✶ Climb the rock's upper bulge. This is a tall route.

65. Unknown (5.5) Climb the broken crack to the rock's top. The rock's quality is poor.

66. Flake Off! (5.8) ✶✶ This route is tall and enjoyable. It offers a lot of good jugs and nubbins.

67. Unknown (5.9) ✶ This dirty route is not recommended.

68. Unknown (5.8) ✶ Climb the wall left of the crack. This rock is tall but mossy.

69. Unknown (5.8) ✶ This route is dirty and mossy and is not highly recommended. The height makes it exciting.

70. Unknown (5.6) ✶ Follow the broken face to the rock's top. The rock is mossy; use caution when descending.

West Fortress

71. Fundamental Physics (5.11b) ✶ Climb the crack splitting the overhanging east face.

72. Unknown (5.11d) ✶✶✶ Use the positive edges to gain the face's overhang. This is a great route, with fluid moves and clean rock.

73. High on Pockets (5.10a) ✶✶✶ See topo. Follow the lowest angle of the face. The route lies behind the tree.

74. Jammin (5.10b) ✶✶ See topo. Climb through the overhang two-thirds of the way up. Use the 2-inch crack as necessary.

75. Sunset (5.9) ✶ See topo. Follow the broken face through two bulges. This route's holds are sharp.

76. South Moon (5.9) ✶✶ Climb over the crescent-shaped break on the rock's south side.

77. Full of Campers (5.9) ✶✶✶ See topo. This route follows an excellent, bulgy face. It is covered with good holds.

RF 1 : 850

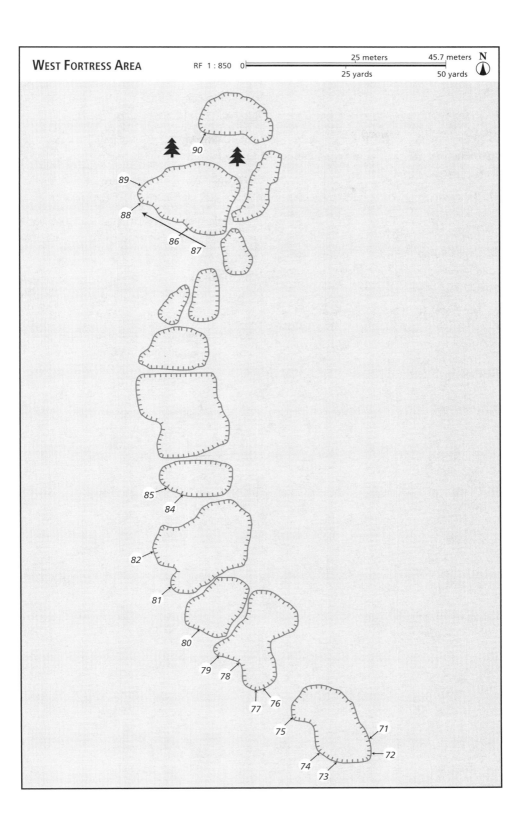

78. Chimney Pipe (5.9) ★★ See topo. Follow the seam in the rock's face. Use long reaches and power to move from jug to jug.

79. TTToday Jr. (5.7) ★★★ See topo. This is a fun face with lots of good edges.

80. Unknown (5.8) ★ Use the good jugs to gain the face's bulge.

81. Unknown (5.6) ★★ Climb the center of the face's bulge. A tall, low-angle ramp takes one to the rock's top.

82. Super Ramp (5.5) ★★ Climb up the bulge's center. This is a fun, airy ramp with huge holds.

83. The Great Traverse (5.7) ★★★ Start at *Full of Campers,* and traverse the west side of multiple rocks to *Super Ramp.* This easy traverse makes a great warm-up route.

84. Unknown (5.8) ★ Climb up the south face's bulge.

85. Unknown (5.5) ★ Use large holds to follow the small seam.

86. Unknown (5.8) ★★ Climb over the angled seam on good holds.

87. Unknown (5.10b) ★ Traverse the block's south side, and move under the fallen tree.

88. Unknown (5.12b) ★★ Climb good jugs to a ceiling. Use power to tackle this strenuous crux.

89. Unknown (5.8) ★★ Follow the seam on the rock's west side. Use good holds to pull over the top.

90. Unknown (5.6) ★ Climb through the bottom overhang, and finish on good edges.

SMITH ROCK STATE PARK

Rock Type	Volcanic Tuff
Quality of Rock (0–5)	5
Maximum Height	350 feet
Ownership	State Park

■ OVERVIEW

A true climbing mecca, Smith Rock State Park is the Northwest's premier climbing destination. Smith Rock is credited with revolutionizing the sport of climbing. It is here, on the edge of the eastern Oregon desert, that the sport route was invented, mastered, and eventually launched onto the worldwide climbing scene.

Within the park one finds volcanic tuff, red tuff, and good hard basalt. The park boasts well over 1,400 routes, including some of the world's most difficult and thrilling sport routes. In addition, steep traditional-style leads, aid lines, gymnastic topropes, and a well-recognized bouldering circuit round

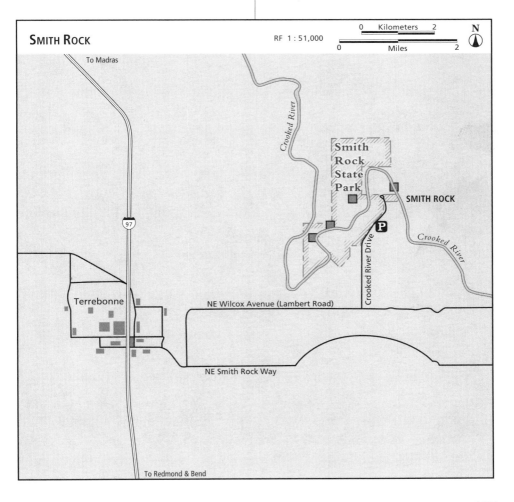

Smith Rock State Park, a true climbing paradise.

out Smith Rock's offerings. The park is well developed with top anchors in place on most routes and good maps and trails to guide the wandering visitor. The level of climbing ranges from beginner to expert; route grades range from 5.1 to 5.14. The tan-colored, nubbin-laden tuff creates delicate and balancy sport routes sure to please even the most fickle climbers. The edgy red tuff and rim-rock basalt provide more secure options for the climber with less-than-rock-hard nerves. Almost all routes grade three quality stars, given the rock's superior quality and feel.

Carry plenty of traditional and sport gear to fully enable all the options the park provides. Climbing can be good year-round, though winters are cold and the summer sun can be too hot for many climbers. The park provides basic services such as drinking water and restrooms.

Tent camping is available in the park for a fee. Free camping is available at Skull Hollow Campground, east of the park, which has restrooms but offers no other services. To find the campground, from the final turnoff into the park, continue east on Northeast

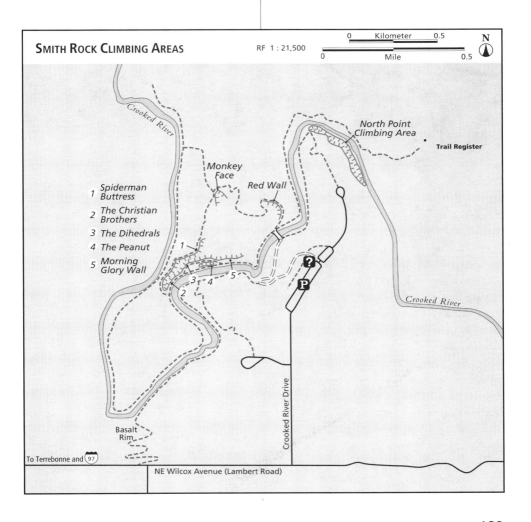

SMITH ROCK CLIMBING AREAS   RF 1 : 21,500

0   Kilometer   0.5

0   Mile   0.5

N

North Point Climbing Area

Trail Register

1 Spiderman Buttress
2 The Christian Brothers
3 The Dihedrals
4 The Peanut
5 Morning Glory Wall

Monkey Face

Red Wall

Crooked River

Crooked River

Basalt Rim

To Terrebonne and 97

Crooked River Drive

NE Wilcox Avenue (Lambert Road)

Smith Rock East Side Climbing Areas

Wilcox Avenue for 2 miles. Turn left onto Smith Rock Way at the stop sign. Drive 0.5 mile and turn left at the stop sign onto North Lone Pine Road. Follow North Lone Pine Road for 3.9 miles, then turn left at the sign into Skull Hollow Campground.

Smith Rock provides a lifetime of adventurous and challenging climbing. The information contained in this guide is not intended to be all-inclusive, but rather serves as a great introduction to the park. Included are the best routes from the most popular and accessible areas. These 159 routes are plenty to keep one busy for many months or even years. *Climber's Guide to Smith Rock,* by Alan Watts, is a thorough supplement to this guide and is highly recommended.

A parking fee is required. The climate is arid, and summer days can be very hot; take

the necessary precautions. The park is very popular and becomes overcrowded during the peak climbing seasons of spring and fall. Avoid Smith Rock during spring break and holidays if you don't like waiting in line to climb.

Finding the crags: From Redmond, drive north on U.S. Highway 97 for 5 miles to Terrebonne. Smith Rock State Park signs lie at each turn, making the park easy to find. In Terrebonne, turn right (east) onto B Avenue. Drive 0.5 mile and turn left (north) onto NE 1st Street, which quickly turns into NE Wilcox Avenue. From the turnoff, drive 1.9 miles and turn left (north) onto Crooked River Drive. Drive 0.5 mile to the state park's main parking area.

Morning Glory Wall

From the parking lot, hike the main trail into the canyon and cross the river bridge. At the base of the towering Picnic Lunch Wall, turn left and follow the river trail for 0.25 mile. After turning the corner, Morning Glory Wall is the first large wall one encounters. The wall hosts several high-quality routes suitable for both beginners and experts. Some routes send the entire wall to its summit. To descend, hike down Cocaine Gully to a technical scramble through a large boulder pile. Cocaine Gully is the first gully east of Morning Glory Wall.

The wall is divided into two main sections. The Churning Buttress area is on the wall's right side and hosts a good selection of expert-level sport routes. The main wall is nearly 200 yards long and is packed with good climbs. Accessibility and route diversity make Morning Glory Wall a popular destination. Routes are listed from right to left.

Morning Glory Wall— Churning Buttress

1. Kings of Rap (5.12d) ✶✶✶ This strenuous sport route is an area classic. Start 10 feet left of the large boulder. Climb through a series of difficult holds to a large ceiling, then traverse right to the outside face. Climb past several more bolts to the top anchors. The crux comes below the large ceiling.

2. Waste Case (5.13b) ✶✶✶ Start 3 feet left of *Kings of Rap*. Power through a strenuous start, then climb past two bolts and traverse up and right. Join *Kings of Rap* to the final bolt below the large ceiling. Traverse left and power through the difficult roof to the outside face. Paste and smear up the blank arête to the top-chains. Four 5.12 cruxes drain even the most powerful climbers. They come at the start, below the roof, just above the roof on the difficult arête, and just above the second-to-the-last bolt.

3. Vicious Fish (5.13d) ✶✶✶ This difficult, sustained route sends the bulging arête on the ceiling's left side. Follow the bolted line up the arête to a bolt just above the roof's left side. Traverse up and right and join *Waste Case*. Send the pumpy, featureless arête to the top-chains. The technical crux comes through a series of desperate hand slaps 10 feet below the roof.

4. Churning in the Wake (5.13a) ✶✶✶ This area classic is one of the most popular routes of its grade. Start 5 feet left of *Vicious Fish,* and climb the pocketed wall past several bolts to the top-chains. Much of the route is sustained 5.12, but the technical crux comes at the last bolt, just below the top anchors.

5. Taco Chips (5.12d) ✶✶✶ Follow a series of winding bolts up the overhanging face. The miniature features on this tall route provide little resting opportunity. The fingery crux comes just above a small 2-inch undercling, halfway up the route.

6. Cool Ranch Flavor 5.11a ✶✶✶ Formerly a desperate runout traditional climb named *Slum Time,* this retro-bolted sport route is now popular. Start 6 feet left of *Taco Chips,* and climb on fun pockets that surround the angled seam. Toward the route's top, move up and right to the top-chains. The pumpy crux comes near the final bolt.

Morning Glory Wall— Main Area

7. Overboard (5.11b) ✷✷✷ This popular sport route follows the chalky seam 20 feet right of the small juniper tree. Climb up a maze of diverse holds to the top anchors. The tricky crux comes at the second-to-the-last bolt. The rarely climbed upper pitch sends crumbly rock through an 11c crux.

8. Magic Light (5.11a) ✷✷ Start by climbing the first three bolts of *Overboard*. At the third bolt, move up and left to a broken seam that almost parallels *Overboard*. Continue up the fun, steep face to the top anchors. The exhausting crux comes at the second-to-the-last bolt.

9. Energy Crisis (5.12b) ✷✷✷ Just right of the small juniper tree, a thin seam with miniature features leads directly to *Magic Light's* top anchors. Pull through a challenging start. Follow the seam, climbing fingery holds to a nice flake below the top anchors. The puzzling crux comes just above the first bolt.

10. Zebra Seam (5.11d R) ✷✷✷ Forty feet left of the juniper tree, a crescent-shaped seam creates a very shallow open book. This sustained mixed-line is bolted, but a few pieces of small traditional gear are used as added security. Much of the route is sustained 5.11, but the technical 11+ crux comes near the top anchors.

11. Zebra Direct (5.11a) ✷✷✷ A fine single-pitch sport route, this line is the preferred variation to *Zebra's* first pitch. Start 10 feet left of *Zebra Seam,* and climb the pocketed face past a series of bolts to the top anchors. The crux comes through the featureless section halfway up the route.

12. Zebra (5.11a) ✷✷ This multi-pitch mixed route sends the entire face to the

wall's summit. The route's first three pitches are delightful, only to be soured by a fourth-pitch scramble up a dirty gully. The route protects well with traditional gear. *Zion* is the more strenuous but preferred route to the wall's top. **Pitch 1:** (5.11a) Climb *Zebra Direct* to its top-belay anchors. *Gumby* can also be climbed, reducing the grade to 5.10b. **Pitch 2:** (5.10a) This pitch sends a beautiful crack up faultless rock. The steep sustained line sits inside a right-facing dihedral. The crux comes at the start of the pitch, through a small bulge above the belay. Jam and stem the sustained line to a nice belay ledge. **Pitch 3:** (5.7) From the belay, step right and climb a large flake crack to a small ledge. Continue up the widening off-width crack to a roomy belay on a large shelf. The crux comes at the start of the pitch, just above the belay. Bring plenty of large traditional gear to protect the wide crack. **Pitch 4:** (4th class) Traverse the ledge left to a dirty gully. Scramble the 4th-class gully to the cliff's summit. Descend via Cocaine Gully.

13. Zion (5.10b) ★★★ This phenomenal line provides a great variation to *Zebra*'s third and fourth pitches. The airy fourth pitch is one of the most exposed and exhilarating free climbs in the park. Besides the easy runout on the third pitch, the route protects well with traditional gear. **Pitch 1:** (5.10b) Climb *Gumby* to the top-belay anchors. *Zebra Direct* can also be sent for an added challenge. **Pitch 2:** (5.10a) Climb the second pitch of *Zebra*. **Pitch 3:** (5.8) Climb the first two-thirds of *Zebra*'s third pitch. Before reaching the large belay ledge, make a fearfully exposed right traverse. Delicately traverse through the crux to an easier ramp-face. Follow the thin seam up and right along the unprotected ramp-face, and continue to a set of belay anchors below the final flake. **Pitch 4:** (5.9) The

exposure on this final pitch is thrilling. Follow the stimulating flake up and left to a ledge below the summit, then scramble easy rock straight up to the cliff's top. The crux comes at the start of the pitch, just above the belay. Descend via Cocaine Gully.

14. Gumby (5.10b) ★★★ This popular sport route climbs the flat wall to huge jugs and joins *Zebra Direct* to the top anchors. Start 10 feet left of *Zebra Direct,* and climb the smooth wall past three bolts to the huge jugs. Move up and right, and join *Zebra Direct* to the top anchors. The thin crux comes above the first bolt.

15. Morning Sky (5.10c) ★★★ A series of bolts makes a linear extension to Gumby. Climb Gumby for 30 feet. At the large jugs, continue straight up to thinner rock above. The fingery crux comes 15 feet below the top anchors.

16. Light On the Path (5.10a) ★★★ This sport route is an area classic. Climb the fun jugs and face holds to the top-chains. The crux comes through the thin section 15 feet below the top anchors.

17. The Outsiders (5.9) ★★★ This fine sport route is relatively new. Its extended height, fun features, and solid rock make it a very popular addition. Start just 5 feet left of *Light On the Path.* Cruise the well-protected, juggy face past several bolts to the top anchors. The crux comes through the obvious thin section between the jugs and pockets.

18. 5 Gallon Buckets (5.8) ★★ By far one of the most climbed routes on the wall, this fun line follows the left-side series of huge jugs. The indiscriminate crux comes through a long reach between huge holds about one-third of the way up the route.

19. Lions Jaw (5.8) ✯✯✯ This route sends a perfect crack in a right-facing dihedral. Hand-jam and stem the flawless rock to a large ledge and top anchors. The route protects well with a standard rack. The climb is fairly sustained, but the actual crux comes at about midroute. Subsequent pitches climb to the rock's summit, but are not included because of the dangerous, loose rock.

20. Tammy Bakker's Face (5.10c) ✯✯✯ This two-pitch sport route climbs a fun ramp and then steep rock to a top anchor. The second pitch is less popular and sees fewer ascents. If climbing the second pitch, use two ropes to rappel from the top anchors. **Pitch 1:** (5.9) This first pitch makes an excellent climb by itself. Start on the face's left side. Use the crack to power through the steep start, then move up and right onto the ramp-face. Follow the bolt line up fun nubbins and pockets to the anchors at the ramp's top. **Pitch 2:** (5.10c) This upper pitch sees much less traffic than the first. Airy exposure and less-than-secure holds make this a thrilling climb though. Continue straight up from the belay, following the bolts through the middle of a shallow groove. Finesse through the difficult bulging crux, then climb up and right to a flake. Traverse the flake up and left through a puzzling 5.10- finish to the top anchors.

Descent via Cocaine Gully

The Peanut

The Peanut is a large rounded rock lying to the left side of Morning Glory Wall. The ease of access and moderate route grades make this a popular pit stop for many climbers. Routes are listed from right to left.

21. Popism (5.11b R) ✱ This is the farthest-right-side route on the Peanut. The 5.11-runout to the first bolt keeps most climbers away; others toprope the line for practice. Follow the bolts up the desperate arête to easier rock above, then scramble the easy ramp to the top anchors. The crux comes between the first and second bolts.

22. Pop Goes the Nubbin
(5.10a) ✱✱ A series of bolts leads up the Peanut's right side to its top anchors. This fun climb serves as an introduction to the 5.10 grade for many climbers. Start to the left side of the void. Pull on small nubbins and edges up the well-protected face to the easier ramp above, then cruise the 5.6 ramp to the top-chains. The crux comes through the steep section above the second bolt.

23. Peanut Brittle (5.8) ✱✱ This fun route lies just to the left of the Peanut's center. The route has two 5.8 sections. The first crux comes above the first bolt; the second comes through the steep bulge two-thirds of the way up.

24. Hop On Pop (5.7) ✱✱ A fun bolt line follows the low-angle face on the Peanut's left side. Climb through the steep crux to the first bolt, then cruise the easy face on fun features to the top-chains.

The Dihedrals

The Dihedrals area arguably provides the greatest concentration of excellent routes within the park. Physically, the area is not large in relation to its neighbors. However, the myriad corners, arêtes, and faces create a high concentration of superb climbs. The Dihedrals can be broken into three sections. On the far right is the Cinnamon Slab area. This low-angle ramp hosts several easy but fun sport and traditional routes, and is a great place for beginners to be introduced to the sport. The center section is made up of steep, flat faces and corners, and the routes are more suitable for intermediate and expert climbers. The steep faces have more pockets and edges, relying less on the infamous spooky nubbins. Some claim this to be the best rock in the park. On the west side, left of the infamous **Chain Reaction,** lies a nice angled slab with mostly intermediate-level routes. You may hear seasoned visitors discuss heading over to Bunny Face. This usually infers the whole left side of the Dihedrals area. These fun, secure climbs rightfully receive plenty of attention.

The Dihedrals— Cinnamon Slab

25. Lichen It (5.7) ★★★ This is the farthest route to the right on the slab. A steep 5.7 start leads to easy cruising up the pocketed ramp-face. Follow the nice, long bolt line to the top anchors.

26. Right Slab Crack (5.5) ★★ Five feet left of *Lichen It,* an obvious crack splits the face. Stem and jam the fun crack up easy rock to *Lichen It'*s shared anchors. The steep crux

comes at the route's start. The line protects well with a standard rack.

27. Easy Reader (5.6) ★★★ A high-quality bolted line sends the protruding ramp just left of *Right Slab Crack.* Scramble up large ledges, and follow a thin seam up and right onto the slab face. Cruise the well-protected ramp to the top-chains.

28. Left Slab Crack (5.4) ★★ Climb the crack 10 feet left of *Easy Reader.* A steep start leads to easy scrambling. Follow the crack to the top anchors shared with *Easy Reader.*

29. Cinnamon & Sugar (5.5) ★★ A bolted line winds through a maze of jumbled rock to a prominent slab. Scramble up large holds for 40 feet to the top of a large rock. Step across to the main slab; climb through the moderate crux, then follow the bolted seam to the top-chains. A 60-meter rope is necessary to lower off.

30. Ginger Snap (5.8) ★★★ This mixed route sends the steep face right of *Cinnamon Slab.* Scramble 30 feet of jumbled rock to a ledge below the steep face. This first 30 feet is easy but is not bolted; use traditional protection to eliminate the runout position. From the ledge, step up to the first bolt. Climb a series of fun nubbins and edges to the top anchors shared with *Cinnamon Slab.* The crux comes just above the first bolt, at midroute.

31. Cinnamon Slab (5.6) ★★★ This is a great traditional climb for the grade. The narrow ramp creates an airy position, and the route protects well with traditional gear. Cruise the fun 5.5. ramp to a flake crack. Climb through the crux, and continue to the top anchors.

The Dihedrals— Center Section

32. Karate Crack (5.10a) ★★★ Climb the nice, steep hand-jam crack to a right-side horizontal crack. Traverse the crack into the hole under the small ceiling, then downclimb a few feet to the top anchors. The jams are solid, but the grade is consistent up the steep face. Protect the final moves to mitigate fall potential for a second climber.

33. Latest Rage (5.12b) ★★★ A beautiful, steep arête lies 15 feet left of *Karate Crack*. A clip-stick is recommended for the first bolt due to the uneven ground below. Start on the right-side wall, and traverse up and left to the first bolt. Slap and pinch, alternating up both sides of the arête to a large hold 10 feet below the top anchors. Carefully send the runout top, up and left, to *Watts Tots*'s shared anchors. The final runout can be protected with a 1½- to 2-inch cam in a small pocket. The two 5.12- cruxes come between the second and third bolts and just above the final bolt.

34. Watts Tots (5.12b) ★★★ This fine sport line weaves its way up the pocketed face left of the *Latest Rage*'s arête. Thought to be impossible when first bolted, the first ascent affirmed the potential of Smith Rock climbing. Much of the route goes at sustained 5.11, but the technical crux comes just above the fifth bolt.

35. Trivial Pursuit (5.10d R) ★★ The outside face of this prominent dihedral hosts two medium-grade routes. The jumbled rock creates a surplus of edges, crimps, and pockets. This is the right-side route. Start on the right-side wall toward the bottom of the stairs, and climb up past one bolt to a series of horizontal ledges. Traverse left to a ramp-ledge, then make a series of easy but exposed moves to the second bolt. This section creates ground-fall potential. Climb through the crux bulge above the second bolt to an easier ramp-face above. Carefully maneuver the runout ramp past two more bolts to the top anchors.

36. Tator Tots (5.10a R) ★★ A near twin to *Trivial Pursuit,* this sport route sends the left side of the prominent face. Climb *Trivial Pursuit* past the first bolt to the horizontal ledge, then traverse left past *Trivial Pursuit* to a bolt on the face's left side. Climb past two bolts, through the crux bulge above the second bolt, and then onto the ramp-face above. Move up and right and join *Trivial Pursuit* at the fourth bolt. Climb the runout face to the top anchors.

37. Latin Lover (5.12a) ★★★ This dihedral's west face hosts two sport routes, and this prominent line receives plenty of traffic. From a block, make an easy first clip. Step onto the steep, pocketed face, and climb through a delightful series of moves past several closely spaced bolts to the top anchors. The technical crux comes above the last bolt through the thin right traverse to the outside arête. Slap and toe a few feet up the arête to the top anchors.

38. Peepshow (5.12b) ★★ *Peepshow* sees far less traffic than its close neighbor. This long, sustained line is a true endurance test. Climb the first four bolts of *Latin Lover.* Utilizing a thin seam, continue up and slightly left to the blank face above. Climb a long series of thin edges past many bolts to the anchors at the rock's top. The first of two 5.11+ cruxes comes through a sustained section two-thirds of the way up; the second follows closely behind. Use two ropes to rappel.

39. Take a Powder (5.12a) ★★★ Two dominant lines send this center face. A true area

classic, *Take a Powder* climbs a fun series of flake holds to a small V-shaped ceiling. Continue up the flake holds to the V's right side. The increasingly steep wall becomes progressively more difficult to the bulging crux above the seventh bolt. Balance through on delicate holds, then continue to the top anchors. The technical crux can be avoided by moving right a few feet.

40. Powder In the Eyes (5.12c) ★★★ This powerful test piece shares the start with *Take a Powder,* then moves up and left at the V-shaped ceiling. Climb *Take a Powder* past three bolts, then power around the ceiling's left side. Maneuver up the shallow arête-spine through two 5.12 cruxes above the fourth and fifth bolts. Continue up the sustained face through a 5.11b move over a small ceiling, then climb past two more bolts to the top anchors.

41. Sunshine Dihedral (5.11d) ★★★ An area classic, this thin inside seam was a sought-after test piece prior to the sport-climbing boom. It sends flawless rock in dihedral between two steep, flat faces. The route's first 30 feet are moderately difficult to protect, but the rest of the route protects well with small wires and cams. The constant grade ranges between 5.10 and 5.11+. The crux comes through a thin tip-jam section 10 feet above the first bolt.

42. To Bolt or Not to Be (5.14a) ★★★ This relentless series of finger pockets and tiny edges helped to put Smith Rock on the worldwide climbing circuit and was the first 5.14 in the United States. It sends the middle of the steep flat face past several bolts to the dihedral's top. The length requires two ropes to rappel. Most of the route grades at sustained 5.12, but the triple 5.13 cruxes come at the fifth, sixth, and ninth bolts.

43. Last Waltz (5.12c) ★★★ This route sends the sustained, prominent arête left of *To Bolt or Not to Be.* Start on the face to the arête's left, and climb *Moondance* through the first three bolts. Traverse up and right to the large ceiling, then move through the technical crux by pulling around the ceiling's right side. Slap and smear up the arête through a 5.12- section at the seventh bolt, then continue on to the top anchors.

44. Moondance (5.11c) ★★★ Fluid moves over perfect rock make this sport route a popular attraction, and three 5.11 cruxes make it a stamina test. They come between the first and second bolts, above the fifth bolt, and then above the eighth bolt. Balance up the delicate edges through the triple cruxes to the top anchors.

45. Wedding Day (5.10b) ★★★ A closely spaced series of bolts sends the right side of an angled arête. Fluid moves, excellent rock, and close bolts make this line a popular warm-up for the more difficult routes in the area. The holds get greasy during high-traffic periods, but that doesn't diminish the route's popularity. Use the arête and good holds to climb the wall to the top anchors. The 5.10-cruxes come before the first bolt and above the fifth bolt.

46. The Flat Earth (5.12a/b) ★★ An attractive line of bolts sits on the overhanging face left of *Wedding Day.* The routes share top anchors. The rock's quality is inferior to its neighbors, originally giving the line a bad reputation. The route stills sees less traffic, resulting in less-polished and stickier holds. Start left of the first bolt, and climb up to a ramp ledge. Step left, and move up to the third bolt. At the third bolt, make a difficult traverse right, through the 5.12- crux, to the arête. Climb good holds up the overhanging arête for 15 feet, and traverse left to the fifth bolt. Power through a pumpy 5.11+ crux to the final bolt, then climb easier rock to the top anchors.

47. Moonshine Dihedral (5.9) ★★★ This popular crack sits tucked back into a steep dihedral. The route protects well with a standard rack. The crux comes through the steep section 15 feet off the ground. Lieback and pull through the crux, then climb easy fun ledges to parallel cracks in the left wall. Jam and stem up the fun cracks through a steep 5.8 section to the top anchors.

48. Heinous Cling (5.12c) ★★★ The steep flat wall left of *Moonshine Dihedral* hosts two excellent sport routes; this is the one on the right. Climb a thin fingertip seam up and right to the first bolt. Traditional protection can be used to limit ground-fall potential. Balance through long reaches between mediocre holds past several bolts to the anchors at the dihedral's top. Some climbers lower off at the anchors midface. This bottom portion grades 5.12a, with the technical crux coming above the fourth bolt. The 5.12c grade includes the route's upper portion and is sent as a single pitch. The crux comes above the seventh bolt. Power through, then climb a sustained 5.11 runout section above the final bolt to the top anchors. All bolts on the route are spaced far apart, making this route more committing than other routes in the same grade. Two ropes are required to lower from the top anchors.

49. Darkness at Noon (5.13a) ★★★ This long sport climb sends the flat face's left side. Most of the route grades consistent 5.11+ through 5.12+. The relentless series of technical moves up the long steep face tests even the fittest climber's endurance. Wander back and forth on tiny holds all the way up the face to the shared anchors at the dihedral's top. A 5.12 crux comes above the third bolt, and the technical 5.12d crux comes above the eighth bolt. Two ropes are required to rappel from the top anchors.

50. Chain Reaction (5.12c) ★★★ This sport route sends the protruding overhang left of *Darkness at Noon*. It instantly became famous when it graced the cover of Watts's guide, and is still one of the most sought-after routes in its grade. Proving the value of combining retro-bolting with acrobatic climbing, the route is credited with validating Smith Rock sport climbing and promoting it on the worldwide scene. Start toward the wall's left side, and climb up and right to the first bolt. Maneuver a tricky series of pockets and arête slaps through the 5.12 crux above the second bolt, then dyno through another 5.12 crux to better holds above the ceiling. Pull through, then clip the top anchors.

The Dihedrals—Left Side

51. Ancylostoma (5.9) ✱✱✱ Climb the steep knobby face to the top of the small rock. The tricky crux on this short route comes through thin pockets above the first bolt.

52. Bookworm (5.7) ✱✱✱ This two-pitch mixed line climbs to the cliff's top. **Pitch 1:** (5.8) Climb the crack on the left side of the small rock; the crux comes at the steep start. The crack protects well, but requires large traditional gear. Climb to the shared anchors with *Ancylostoma*. **Pitch 2:** (5.6) From the belay, follow the well-protected bolt line up the knobby face to anchors near the cliff's top. Rappel the route in two pitches.

53. Bunny Face (5.7) ✱✱✱ This route is an area classic. Climb the amusing ramp on solid nubbins and edges to a ledge and the top

anchors. The crux comes two-thirds of the way up the route. From the top-belay, it is possible to traverse right and join the second pitch of *Bookworm* to the cliff's top.

54. Rabbit Stew (5.7) ✱✱ This fun traditional climb follows a finger-jam crack in a left-facing dihedral. The route protects well with traditional gear. The barely noticeable crux comes about one-third of the way up the route. Top anchors are in place at the crack's top.

55. Lycopodophyta (5.7) ✱✱✱ Not pictured. This amusing line follows the left-side fingertip crack, up the ramp-face left of *Rabbit Stew.* Fun face holds and solid jams add to the route's quality. The crack can be sewn up with small to medium traditional gear.

56. Helium Woman (5.9) ✱✱ Climb up edges and nubbins through a series of well-

spaced bolts on the face's right side. The steep start is sustained, but leads to easier climbing as the angle drops.

57. Captain Xenolith (5.10a) ✶ The upper portion of this sport route is good, but an awkward crux between the first and second bolts diminishes its quality. Climb the steep rock past the first bolt, then traverse up and left through the awkward, stretchy crux. Continue a short series of difficult moves to good holds up the angled face.

58. Deteriorata (5.8) ✶ This crack continues to become better as it is cleaned, yet it sees few ascents. The line protects well with a standard rack. Stem and jam good rock

through the crux roof, then continue up steep rock to easier climbing above. The rock quality deteriorates higher on the route, which shares top anchors with *Captain Xenolith*.

59. Go Dog Go (5.12c) ✶✶ This highly visible and popular line cranks the large overhang on the farthest-left face. Start on the face's left side, and climb up and right through a bulge to the outside face. Power up a variety of slopers, edges, and good jugs to the top anchors at the rock's top. The first crux comes above the fourth bolt, the second on thin holds below the second-to-the-last bolt.

Christian Brothers

The Christian Brothers area is composed of a massive chunk of volcanic tuff and hosts a plentiful selection of sport and traditional routes. It lies between the Dihedrals and Asterisk Pass and takes about twenty minutes to reach from the main parking lot. The Christian Brothers rock is broken into three sections. Prophet Wall is the rightmost area. This rounded, featureless buttress has several difficult sport routes and is best suited for expert climbers. Testament Slab hosts the middle set of climbs and is a worthy stop. On the far left is the Combination Blocks area. It has a tight concentration of midgrade routes, making it well suited for intermediate climbers.

Christian Brothers— Prophet Wall

60. Rawhide (5.11d) ✳✳ This short but difficult route winds its way up the steep upper face. Pull over a small roof. Make a smeary hand traverse left, then climb tiny edges to the top anchors.

61. Smooth Boy (5.13b) ✳✳ Climb steep rock to a series of 5.12- hand smears below the large angled roof. Power to the right-side face through the difficult crux on a one-finger pocket and tiny edge. Tiptoe up the blank wall to the top anchors. Reduce rope drag by protecting the roof with a long sling.

62. Choke On This (5.12d) ✳✳ This difficult line climbs through a series of small roofs. It starts 15 feet downhill from *Smooth Boy*. Follow the seam to the sustained 5.12 crux between the second and fifth bolts. Pull over

another roof on good holds, then balance up small 5.11+ edges to the top anchors.

63. Dreamin (5.12a R) ★★★ This long, sustained route is a real fitness test. The spacey bolts and constant grade make an exciting and committing line. Traverse up and left to the first bolt. Balance through the crux on insecure holds to a small ceiling, and pull through to the flat face above. Send tiny edges to a large 5.11 roof, then make a long lock-off to mediocre holds on the outside face. Pull around and climb the face to the top anchors. Reduce rope drag by protecting the roof with a long sling.

64. Boy Prophet (5.12b R) ★★★ This route shares the same start with *Dreamin*. The insecure crux comes past the first bolt, but the sustained climbing can lead to power failure toward the route's top. Climb up and left past three bolts to a good ledge below a small bulge. Pull over and fight through a 5.11+ section above the next bolt. Continue on insecure holds to the top anchors below the large ceiling.

65. Rude Boys (5.13c) ★★★ This route provides an insanely difficult variation to the start of *Boy Prophet*. Pull through the seemingly impossible cruxes above the first bolt and at the third bolt. At the fourth bolt, send the right side of the slap arête and join *Boy Prophet* at the fifth bolt.

66. Rude Femmes (5.13c/d) ★★★ From the start of *Rude Boys,* power the same impossible sequence to the fourth bolt. Climb up and left through a sustained 5.12 section onto the flat outside wall. Follow the bolts paralleling to the right of *Scarface*. The entire upper face goes at sustained 5.11+/5.12-. Consequently, the route sees few ascents.

67. Scarface (5.14a) ★★★ This classic line was one of the first 5.14s in the entire United States. The insanely difficult line powers the steep overhang on tiny pockets and edges to the sustained 5.11 arête above. Good luck.

Christian Brothers— Testament Slab Area

68. Heresy (5.11c) ★★ This newer sport route receives a lot of attention. It sends a positive flake rim through the aggressively overhanging left side of Prophet Wall. A clip-stick is recommended to decrease the likeli-hood of landing flat on your back. Traverse a fun rim through the steep overhang, then power up the overhanging wall to the diffi-cult crux at the last bolt. High-step and make a desperate move to great holds at the top anchors.

69. Wartley's Revenge (5.11b) ★★★ This overhanging crack is an area classic. To this day, it is a sought-after test piece for all aspir-ing traditional climbers. The route protects well with small to medium cams and wires. Climb the 5.10 ramp through a shaky series of stems to a small 5.10- overhang. Power through the right side on positive holds, and continue through another 5.10- roof to the seam below the top anchors. Jam to the seam's top, then make a desperate face move through the technical crux to the top-chains. Placing gear through the constantly over-hanging face pumps even the fittest climbers.

70. The Right Side of the Beard (5.7) ★★ A nice crack separates the right side of the Beard from the main wall. The short route protects well with traditional gear. The crux comes at the bulge halfway up.

71. Risk Shy (5.12a) ★ This toprope can be set up by climbing any of the other routes that gain the Beard's top. The right, outside arête of the Beard makes a challenging short climb. Slap, pinch, and smear up the feature-less arête to the top anchors. The crux comes through the steep section halfway up.

72. Golgotha (5.11b R) ★★ This thin inside seam separates Testament Slab from the main wall. Solid gear placement is difficult, making this a better toprope than lead. Jam and stem the thin seam to two bolts at the route's top. Climb past the bolts, through the crux on tiny holds, to the top anchors shared with *Barbecue the Pope.*

73. Barbecue the Pope (5.10b) ★★★ A wild, twisting line of bolts sends the right side of Testament Slab. Stretch across good holds up the steep face to the top anchors. The pumpy line has two 5.10- cruxes, but many climbers have a power failure at the last bolt. The first crux comes below the third bolt, and the second comes between the fifth and sixth bolts.

74. New Testament (5.10a) ★★★ This tra-ditional route sends the steep crack splitting the left side of the slab's face. The route pro-tects well with a standard rack. No single move is difficult, but placing gear through the series of bulges makes this more strenu-ous than other routes of the grade. Climb the chunky crack through a small 5.8 roof, and continue on through a pumpy 5.7 bulge halfway up. Jam and work face holds to the 5.9 crux at the bottom of the V. Protect the crux well, then pull through on insecure holds to easier climbing and the top anchors shared with *Barbecue the Pope.*

75. Revelations (5.9) ★★★ The next three sport routes send Testament Slab's south face. Follow a series of bolts up the steep right-side arête. Above the route's midpoint, move up and left and climb the block's center to the top-chains. The tricky crux comes above the first bolt. Utilize holds on both sides of the arête to pull through.

76. Irreverence (5.10a) ★★★ This fun line climbs the middle of the chunky face. A high-step start leads to the first bolt. Continue on fun holds to the spooky thin

crux above the third bolt. Tiptoe through to
easier climbing, and join *Revelations* to the
shared top anchors.

77. Nightingale's On Vacation (5.10b) ★★
A bolt line starts on the far left side of the

slab's south face. Follow a few bolts up the
left-side arête to a ledge, then step up to a
steep section of rock. The crux comes above
the first bolt on this upper portion. Climb
the fun face past several more bolts to the
top anchors.

Christian Brothers— Combination Blocks

78. Overnight Sensation (5.11a) ✶✶ This short sport route sends the steep face of Combination Blocks. The long spacing between the first and second bolts can lead to a ground fall; take the necessary precautions. Climb the lower 5.10 block past three bolts to a good resting ledge. Traverse up and right through the thin 5.11- crux to the ramp on the block's top. Scramble the easy ramp up and left to the top anchors.

79. Bum Rush the Show (5.13b) ✶✶✶ A bolted line follows the brown streaks above Combination Blocks. From the top of the blocks, step onto the overhanging rounded wall. Pull on pockets and tiny edges up the featureless overhanging wall to the top anchors. Much of the route goes at sustained 5.12, but the technical 5.13 crux comes above the fourth bolt.

80. Tinker Toy (5.9 X) ✶✶ This toprope climbs the fun left-side arête of Combination Blocks' main face. Slap and lieback the arête while utilizing good face holds to help the ascent. The crux comes halfway up the top block.

81. Double Trouble (5.10b) ✶✶✶ An area classic, this exhilarating line receives lots of attention. Follow a series of well-spaced bolts up the narrow south side of Combination Blocks. The exciting crux comes through an intimidating lieback up the top block.

82. Bowling Alley (5.5) ✶ A wide dirty crack separates Combination Blocks from the main wall. Inside the rock gully, climb the right-side crack that lies next to *Double Trouble*. The crux comes at the separation between the blocks. At the top block, squeeze up and behind into the chimney. Thrash up the chimney to the block's top.

83. Toys In the Attic (5.9) ✶ Inside the rock gully, opposite the *Bowling Alley,* a wide crack leads to a large roof. Climb the unpleasant, debris-filled crack to the roof. Traverse a hand crack down and left to *Hesitation Blues*'s top anchors.

84. Hesitation Blues (5.10b) ✷✷✷ A thin crack splits the steep wall left of Combination Blocks. The route protects well with a standard rack. Climb the thin seam past a small ledge to the flake crack. Jam the flake crack moving up and right, and follow it to the top anchors.

85. Ring of Fire (5.11d) ✷✷✷ This popular sport route receives constant action during peak climbing seasons. The slew of chalky holds hides the true complexity of the difficult crux. Maneuver fun holds past two bolts to a small overhang, then pull through and tackle the perplexing crux above the third bolt. Continue up relatively sustained rock to the top anchors.

86. Unknown (5.10a) ✷✷✷ Left of *Ring of Fire* a sport route loosely follows the left-side ridgeline. Climb chunky holds through a series of pumpy bulges. Close to *Ring of Fire*'s top anchors, pull over the ridge and climb easy rock to the top anchors.

87. Self Preservation (5.10a) ✷✷✷ Hand traverse the diagonal crack up and right to the top anchors shared with *Hesitation Blues*. This fun crack protects well with traditional gear. The exciting crux comes through a series of foot smears and fingertip jams through the thin part of the crack. The original line, called *Toy Blocks,* leaves the nice crack and sends dirty flakes to *Dancer*'s top anchors.

88. Dancer (5.7) ✷✷✷ The ramp-face on the far left side of the Combination Blocks area hosts two fun and easy sport routes. This climb follows a series of well-spaced bolts up the ramp's right side to top anchors shared with *Jete.* Cruise large holds and knobs past five bolts, then climb easy rock up and left to the top anchors. The indiscriminate crux comes on smaller nubbins past the fourth bolt.

89. Jete (5.8) ✷✷✷ Start near the bottom of *Dancer.* Climb easy holds up and left past several bolts to a low-angle section halfway up the block. Cruise easy rock between a long bolt spacing, and join *Dancer* to the top anchors. The crux comes just above the third bolt.

Spiderman Buttress

Embedded within the west-side crags, between Asterisk Pass and Monkey Face, this stunning buttress attracts more than its share of attention. The buttress is accessed by following the river trail to the west side or by shortcutting over Asterisk Pass. From the main parking area, the total hike takes about one-half hour. The buttress hosts several high-quality traditional routes and mixed climbs. Several routes ascend multiple pitches to the buttress's top. To descend, hike south to the first gully and follow a descent trail to the rock's base.

90. Main Street Stroll (5.5) ✶ Just right of *Spiderman*'s original start lies this short and easy crack. It protects well with traditional gear and makes a good route to learn to place traditional gear on. The rock is great, but the lack of any excitement makes this a rather mundane climb. Climb through the steep crux at the route's start, then scramble up the easy ramp and crack to the top anchors.

91. Spiderman (5.7) ✶✶✶ This two-pitch traditional route is an area classic. **Pitch 1:** (5.7) Start to the right side of the cone-shaped rock, and climb the well-protecting crack up an easy ramp for 40 feet. Continue past a set of belay anchors to the steeper rock above. Climb 30 feet, over a small bulge to the spacious belay ledge. The exciting 5.7 crux comes at the bulge directly below the belay ledge. **Pitch 2:** (5.7) Step right from the belay slab to an obvious crack in the steep wall. Climb the well-protecting crack to a large roof, then make a series of exposed liebacks to pull around the roof's right side. Scramble up easier rock to the buttress's top.

92. Squashed Spider (5.7) ✶✶ A series of bolts makes this once-runout ramp a delightful climb. The route sends the middle of the lower cone-shaped buttress; the crux comes at the route's start. Cruise the fun ramp past a series of bolts to the top anchors.

93. Spiderman Variation (5.7) ✶✶✶ The jumbled crack on the lower cone-shaped buttress's left side makes a nice variation start to *Spiderman*'s first pitch. The crack protects well with traditional gear. Climb jumbled easy rock for 30 feet, then stem the knobby walls and jam the crack another 20 feet to the top anchors. Stop here, or join *Spiderman*'s first pitch and continue another 30 feet to the belay ledge atop its first pitch.

94. Widow Maker (5.9 R) ✶ This two-pitch traditional route climbs to the buttress's top and provides a lower quality alternative to *Spiderman*. Gear placements can be strenuous and are generally more difficult to make. **Pitch 1:** (5.9) Start on the *Spiderman Variation* route. Climb 25 feet, then step left to a crack system in the main wall, and climb solid rock past a 2-foot ceiling. Move around the ceiling's right side, then climb a 5.9 ramp for 20 feet to another small ceiling. Move up through the V-shaped notch following the crack to an exciting flake above. Make a strenuous series of moves through the over-hanging crux-flake to the belay ledge above. **Pitch 2:** (5.5) Follow a series of cracks up easy rock to the buttress's top.

95. Best Left to Obscurity (5.8) ✶ This route's original line follows a maze of dogleg flakes and roofs, making it an unpleasant experience with horrible rope drag. The original crux, which lies higher on the route, is 5.10a. A more popular line follows the route's bottom 50 feet to a shared set of anchors with *Explosive Energy Child*. Start on a small boulder left of *Spiderman Variation,* and step across to an obvious flake. Climb the crescent-shaped ramp flake for 50 feet to the shared top anchors. The unthrilling crux

comes at the route's start. The route protects well with a standard rack of traditional gear.

96. More or Lester (5.10c) ✹✹ A steep nubbin-covered face lies 6 feet right of *Explosive Energy Child*. This strenuous toprope is sure to test one's pinching and balancing skills. The balancy crux comes toward the route's start.

97. Explosive Energy Child (5.10d R) ✹✹✹ This area classic is a true finger test piece. It is a mixed route requiring both sport gear and small traditional protection. Difficult traditional placements and runout bolt spacings make this R-rated route a less-than-good lead for the timid climber. Jam a crack for 10 feet to a V-shaped feature. Step left and balance through a series of delicate moves to a slanted crack, then follow the thin seam to the top anchors. The crux comes just before the second bolt.

98. Out of Harm's Way (5.8) ✹✹✹ This mixed route follows a lieback crack to a ledge on top of the detached flake, then tackles the splendid wall above. Jam and stem the 5.7 crack to the flake's top. This section protects well with larger traditional gear. From the block's top, follow a series of closely spaced bolts up splendid and exposed rock to the top anchors. The steep crux comes halfway up the upper wall.

99. In Harm's Way (5.7) ✹✹✹ This delightful line shares the same start with *Out of Harm's Way*. Stem the 5.7 crack all the way to the block's top. Follow the bolted line up the ramp-face to the top anchors. The crux comes through the thinner section three-quarters of the way up the route.

100. Little Feat (5.10b) ✹✹ This bold line sends the entire face in one long pitch. The route protects well with traditional gear.

Scramble jumbled rock for 30 feet to an obvious right-facing corner. Stem and jam a series of parallel cracks to a small ceiling 30 feet from the cliff's top. Lieback through the fingertip crux, and pull through to an easy exit ramp. Follow the ramp up and right to the cliff's top.

101. Cornerstone (5.11d) ✶✶ This two-pitch mixed line requires both sport and traditional gear. **Pitch 1:** (5.7) Climb the first half of *Little Feat* to a belay ledge on top of a detached block. **Pitch 2:** (5.11d) From the belay ledge, climb the steep 5.11- left-side face, following a thin seam for 15 feet. Step left and pull up and over to a nice ledge on the outside face, then climb the exposed and thrilling arête past a series of bolts. At the last bolt, traverse to the right-side face and climb through to the cliff's top. The last 15 feet requires small traditional gear to protect. The stimulating crux comes just before the final bolt on the outside face.

102. Cornerstone Variation (5.10a) ✶✶ This variation of the first pitch is actually the original line. Start 10 feet left of *Cornerstone,* and climb an inset crack up a steep ramp for 25 feet to an overhanging inset crack. Thrash through the awkward crux, then step left to the outside face of the detached flake. Maneuver up the knobby face to a ledge and the top-chains. Lower off, or climb *Death Takes a Holiday* or the rest of *Cornerstone's* second pitch to the cliff's top.

103. Death Takes a Holiday (5.12a) ✶✶ A thrilling but neglected line follows a series of bolts up the steep outside face above *Cornerstone Variation*. The powerful crux comes just above the final bolt below the cliff-top. The route can be accessed by first climbing *Cornerstone Variation* or by rappelling from above.

Ben questioning his sanity on the West Face of Monkey Face.

Monkey Face

Monkey Face is one of the most popular features in the park. It is accessed by hiking around the river trail or over Asterisk Pass to the west-side crags. Or, it can be accessed by hiking past Red Wall and over Misery Ridge. This stunning tower is 350 feet tall on its west face, and many of its routes climb to the summit. Two ropes are needed for the rappel. To descend, rappel from the summit anchors to a rappel station on a large ledge on the rock's southeast side. The block on the ledge's right side has robust rappel anchors and rings. Use a double-rope rappel and descend the open air to the base of the *Pioneer Route*.

Monkey Face—West Side

104. West Face Variation (5.8) ★★★ This true area classic scales the west-face wall just right of Monkey Face over three long pitches. It protects well with traditional gear. Bring long runners for protection to reduce rope drag through the myriad ceilings and corners. The route has a number of second- and third-pitch variations. Most climbers prefer the line detailed here. **Pitch 1:** (5.8) Locate the large ceiling 40 feet off the ground. Directly below it, a large crack diagonals up and left and ends on stacked blocks. Climb the diagonal crack up and left for 30 feet to the top of the stacked blocks. The pushy crux lies halfway up the diagonal crack. Climb a steep but easy inside corner for 15 feet, then muscle past two bulges to a large belay ledge. **Pitch 2:** (5.5) From the belay, climb an easy ramp for 50 feet to the base of a large ceiling. Scramble up and right around the ceiling, then traverse up and left to a belay. This large turn in the route creates extreme rope drag. Place protection carefully,

n the thin seam, moving right of
the top anchors shared with
The crux comes between
d bolts.

2c) ★★★ A tall bolted
ll left of *Astro*
at the route's start
~s away. Balance
veral bolts to
lake a series
?- crux at
nish the

This route
top of Monkey
over six airy and
exciting pitches, but
most climbers stop after
the first pitch, which is
all that is described here.
The first pitch is mixed
and requires sport and
small traditional protec-
tion. The route starts
directly below the 2-
foot ceiling 40 feet up.
Climb through a diffi-
cult series of small edges
and nubbins past four
bolts to a thin seam
below the ceiling.

108. West Face (5.12a, C2 or C2) ✶✶✶ The most phenomenal aid line in the park, *West Face* sends 350 feet of mostly overhanging blank rock. The first pitch goes free at 5.12a or is easily aid-climbed with small traditional gear; the next three pitches follow a continuous bolted ladder to Monkey Face's summit. This is an old line, and bolts have been known to pop out. A clip-stick is highly recommended to work past missing bolts. **Pitch 1:** (5.12a, C2 or C2) Aid-climb past five bolts to a thin crack splitting the wall's left side. Free-climb the strenuous and unrelenting crack to the belay, or aid-climb it with small wires. When freed, the technical crux comes through the blank section 50 feet up. Power failures frequently occur while trying to place gear on the shaky fingertip jams. **Pitch 2:** (C2) Climb the bolted ladder up the overhanging featureless wall to the belay just above the rounded bulge. Gear removal can be difficult for the second climber given the overhanging grade. If there is a third climber in the party and he or she is jumarring the lines, be prepared for an exhilarating swing into open air when unclipping from the belay. **Pitch 3:** (C2) Continue the sustained line to the first comfortable belay in the West Face cave. Enjoy the airy and thrilling exposure. **Pitch 4:** (C1) Toward the north side of the cave, a bolt-ladder sends the large overhang face. Climb the short bolted ladder through the overhang and onto the ramp-face above, then scramble up the ramp-face to Monkey Face's summit. Communication between climbers on the summit and in the cave is difficult to impossible, which results in an increased probability of serious mistakes. Walkie-talkies or other communication devices are highly recommended.

109. Sheer Trickery (5.12b) ✶✶✶ This mixed route starts just left of *West Face* and loosely follows the left-side arête. Maneuver a strenuous start past three bolts. Past the third bolt, traverse up and right and climb the *West Face* crack for 30 feet. Just prior to the 5.11+ crux in the *West Face* crack, traverse left and rejoin the bolted line. Power through the flat, steep 5.12- section to the ramp arête above. Climb past two more bolts, then break up and left before the 1-foot horizontal bulge. This leads directly to the top anchors. The technical crux comes between the first and second bolts.

110. The Backbone (5.13a) ✶✶✶ This is a relentless multi-pitch sport route that sends the northwest arête in its entirety. The exposed position and perfect moves make this area classic a sought-after test piece. **Pitch 1:** (5.6) From the north side, traverse the jumbled ledge to the belay anchors on the northwest arête. **Pitch 2:** (5.13a) Climb the thrilling arête past several bolts to an anchor belay. Larger ledges and face holds on either side of the arête are of good use. The relentless crux comes at the last bolt below the belay anchors. **Pitch 3:** (5.12a) From the belay, traverse right, moving onto the flat, overhanging west face. Join the *West Face* route, and send the steep face into the *West Face* cave. **Pitch 4:** (5.12a) Start 20 feet right of *West Face*'s fourth pitch. Make an exposed move onto the steep overhanging wall, and climb past several bolts to Monkey Face's summit.

111. North Face (5.12a) ✶✶✶ This phenomenal multi-pitch mixed line sends the flake seam splitting the north face. Pitches 2 and 3 are best combined into one long, sustained pitch. A 60-meter rope is necessary to combine the pitches. **Pitch 1:** (5.6) From the north side, traverse the jumbled ledge to the belay anchors on the northwest arête. **Pitch 2:** (5.11b) Climb the arête past several bolts until it is possible to traverse left into the flake crack. Jam and lieback the fingertip flake to a hanging belay. The crux comes at the right turn in the flake 10 feet below the belay anchors. **Pitch 3:** (5.12a) Continue up the flake seam until it ends, then traverse up and right into the West Face cave. **Pitch 4:** (5.11b) Climb the top pitch of *West Face* to the rock's summit. The juggy overhanging face goes free at 5.11b.

Monkey Face—East Side

112. Spank the Monkey (5.12a R) ★★★
This phenomenal test piece follows a spacey bolted line up the northeast arête. The difficult crux comes above the third bolt. Maneuver through features on either side of the steep arête to the top anchors. Small traditional protection is helpful to cut the runout above the final bolt.

113. East Face (5.13c/d) ★★★ This multi-pitch mixed climb follows the crack on the right side of the east face. The perfect rock and airy exposure make this a true thriller, though the top pitch is hardly worth the bother. Two ropes are needed to rappel from the belay anchors at the top of the first pitch. On redpoint attempts, protection is usually pre-placed. **Pitch 1:** (5.13c/d) Jam the fingertip seam past a set of anchors to the top-belay on the ramp-face. The anchors lie 40 feet below the summit. The double 5.13- cruxes come toward the top of the seam and just below the anchors. **Pitch 2:** (5.10b) Climb the ramp past a few bolts to the steep overhang above. Free the bolted ladder on positive holds to the right-side ramp, and scramble to the rock's summit.

114. Just Do It (5.14c) ★★★ This incredible line is one of the most difficult and sought-after climbs in the world. Climb the ridiculously difficult face in one long pitch. The near-impossible crux balances bullet-size pockets where each is just out of reach from the other. The crux comes around the third-to-the-last bolt near the route's top. The bottom half of the route grades 5.13c.

115. Megalithic (5.12d) ★★★ This sport route starts a few feet left of *Just Do It*. Solid holds provide decent rests between sections of difficult rock. The crux comes at the last bolt before the anchors.

116. Rising Expectations (5.11d) ★★★ A beautiful crack splits the left side of the east face. The route protects well with a standard rack. Jam the fingertip crack up the steep flat face to the top anchors. The crux comes through the bulge at the route's top.

1st Rappel Station

117

2nd Rappel Station

113

110

117

3rd Rappel Station

116

115

111

114

113

112

117

110

2nd Rappel
Station

117

117

117. Pioneer Route (5.7, C1) ✭✭✭ This multi-pitch line on the south side of Monkey Face is the standard route to the summit. Given its simplicity and exciting exposure, it is very popular. The route becomes a nonstop line of traffic during peak climbing season. **Pitch 1:** (4th class) Scramble an easy ramp to the steeper corner. **Pitch 2:** (5.5) Make a series of moves to the notch between the pillar and the cliff. Step left onto the south face, and climb to a large belay ledge called Bohn Street. **Pitch 3:** (C1) Aid the airy bolted ladder to a roomy belay in the south-side cave. **Pitch 4:** (5.7) Step out of the right side of the cave, and make a series of thrilling, exposed moves on good holds to a large belay ledge. Close bolt spacings make it possible to aid the unnerving moves out of the cave. **Pitch 5:** (5.4) Traverse around the boulder, and make an easy scramble to the rock's summit.

Ian puts gravity to the test on the *Pioneer Route* on Smith Rock's popular Monkey Face.

Red Wall

The Red Wall climbing area towers over the Misery Ridge Trail as it switchbacks to the summit ridge. It lies 300 yards to the north of Picnic Lunch Wall. From the main parking area, hike the trail to the river bridge. On the far side of the bridge, continue straight up a steep trail to Picnic Lunch Wall's right side, and continue right for 200 yards to Red Wall's base. The wall supports several medium-grade sport routes and also hosts a few high-quality multi-pitch traditional climbs.

118. Finger Puppet (5.10a) ★★ On Red Wall's far left side, a distinct oval-shaped rock, called Bill's Flake, sits atop a large ledge. This sport route climbs the middle of the flake to anchors at its top. The short crux sequence comes above the first bolt on the flake. There

are two ways to reach the flake's bottom. On the far left side of the ledge, scramble easy rock, then move right along the ledge to the flake's bottom. Or, the route can be sent as a mixed line by climbing the nice crack directly below it to reach the flake's bottom, then continuing through to the top anchors. The crack protects well with traditional gear.

119. Phantasmagoria (5.10b) ★★ This route extends off *Finger Puppet* and climbs the steep wall above Bill's Flake. Climb *Finger Puppet* to the second bolt on the flake. Past the second bolt, move up and right and climb the fun, featured face past several bolts to the top anchors. The balancy crux comes at the third bolt from the top.

120. Pop Art (5.10c) ★★ A short block just to the right of Bill's Flake hosts two sport routes; this unmemorable line is the left-side route. Climb pockets and edges past three

bolts to the top anchors. The crux comes on a series of sloping holds between the second and third bolts.

121. Dances With Clams (5.10a) ★★ A better route than its neighbor, this sport line climbs the block's right side. Move up good edges and flake holds through a fun bulging crux above the third bolt, then continue up the steep rock to the top anchors.

122. Super Slab (5.6) ★★★ This multi-pitch traditional route climbs two fun ramps to the cliff's top. Solid protection, great rock, and fun moves make this one of the best routes of its grade. To descend, rappel the route in two pitches. **Pitch 1:** (5.6) Follow the right-side crack up the ramp-face for 70 feet to a large belay ledge. The crack protects well with large traditional gear. Most of the pitch grades sustained 5.5. **Pitch 2:** (5.3) From the belay above the lower ramp, traverse left across a large broken ledge to the base of the upper prominent ramp. This easy, short pitch can be protected with traditional gear, but few good placements are available. **Pitch 3:** (5.6) This top pitch sends the obvious ramp on the wall's left side, and ends at the cliff's top. The pitch protects well with a standard rack, and the exposure and enjoyable moves make this one of the best single pitches on the Red Wall. Top anchors are in place to rappel.

123. Two Perfect Stars (5.9) ★★ A prominent tan-colored face lies 50 feet to the right
of *Super Slab*'s start. This fun sport route
climbs through the huge jugs on the face's
left side. The double 5.8+ cruxes come at the
fourth and eighth bolts. This is a nice, long,
fun route, but the rock quality diminishes the
overall experience.

**124. Randomly Focused Thoughts for Brief
Periods of Time** (5.12a) ★★★ This sport
route sends the wall 10 feet left of the
prominent crack in the middle of the face.
Good rock and fun technical moves make
this an enjoyable line. Climb an edgy ramp
then steeper rock to the third bolt. Traverse
up and right to an arête feature, then make a
short series of moves up the shallow arête

and traverse left across the blank face to good holds. Climb enjoyable and easier rock to the top anchors. The two 5.11+ technical cruxes come at the traverses above the third bolt and at the fifth bolt.

125. If Six Were Nine (5.10b) ★★

A thin diagonal seam splits the face's right side. Recently retro-bolted, this line now makes a good sport route. Start at the crescent-shaped roof at the rock's bottom, and maneuver through the bouldery start to better holds above. Climb past several bolts to the flat face above, then follow the thin seam up the steep face to a good ledge below the top anchors. Step left to the shared anchors. The crux comes through a sustained series of thin holds between the third and fifth bolts.

126. Ride the Lightning (5.11b) ★★★

This popular sport routes climbs the steep right side of the face. Surmount a large block, then make a few moves and stretch to the first clip. Continue up side-pulls and small edges to the top anchors. The technical crux comes at the steep section above the second bolt.

127. Chairman Mao's Little Red Book

(5.11a) ★★★ This two-pitch traditional route climbs an easy jumbled ramp then a steep inside corner to the top anchors shared with *If Six Were Nine*. **Pitch 1:** (5.6) Climb easy holds up the jumbled crack in the dihedral, just right of *Ride the Lightning*. The crux comes through the steep section at the pitch's start. Continue up an easy jumbled ramp to a webbing sling belay. Bring fresh webbing in case it needs to be replaced. **Pitch 2:** (5.11a) Step left into the steep dihedral. Fingertip jam and stem the flat walls up the short pitch to a large ledge, then move left to the top anchors. This top pitch requires small wires and cams to protect. The crux comes through the featureless section toward the dihedral's top.

128. Fingers of Fate (5.10d) ★★★

This two-pitch traditional route starts on the right side of the jumbled ramp, 20 feet to the right of *Chairman Mao's Little Red Book*. Two ropes are needed to rappel from the anchors atop the second pitch. **Pitch 1:** (5.7) Climb good holds up the jumbled crack to the webbing belay at the top of *Chairman Mao's Little Red Book*'s first pitch. This pitch protects well with a standard rack. **Pitch 2:** (5.10d) Step right, under the small roof, and into the crack system. Climb the steep crack on good holds for 15 feet through a small bulge. Follow the crescent-shaped crack up and left, and through a small 5.10- ceiling. Pull around the ceiling, and continue traversing the crack to its end. Climb straight up past one bolt to the top anchors; the technical crux comes at this bolt.

129. Sole Survivor (5.11b) ★★★

This sport route sends the knobby face 10 feet right of *Fingers of Fate*. Climb up the face through a thin 5.10- section above the first bolt, then continue up the steep face past several bolts until it is possible to step right to a solid flake. Pull upward, then tackle the thin, bulging 5.11- crux at the second-to-the-last bolt. Climb a few more feet to the top anchors.

130. Let's Face It (5.10b) ★★★

This high-quality bolted line starts toward the face's left side and diagonals up and right to a belay ledge. Sequence up good holds on perfect rock past several bolts to the top anchors. The steep crux comes above the second-to-the-last bolt.

131. Peking (5.8) ★★

This three-pitch traditional route follows the left-side crack of two prominent parallel cracks that gain Red Wall's top. The first pitch climbs a perfect hand-jam crack. Many climbers send just the bottom of the first pitch and lower at the first set of anchors. To descend, scramble to the cliff's top and the Misery Ridge Trail. Hike to the right, into the gully, and follow Misery Ridge Trail to the cliff's base. The route protects well with a standard rack. **Pitch 1:** (5.8) Traverse the hand crack up and left to a perfect crack splitting the steep face. Jam the flawless crack to a set of top anchors, and either lower off or continue up easier, jumbled rock for 30 more feet to a belay ledge. **Pitch 2:** (5.8) From the belay, pull over a strenuous bulge and move into the obvious crack system. Much of the middle pitch goes at sustained 5.7. Climb the long pitch to a good belay ledge 30 feet below the cliff's top. A 60-meter rope is recommended for this pitch. **Pitch 3:** (4th class) Move along the belay ledge up and right until an easy 4th-class scramble leads to the top.

132. Moscow (5.6) ★★★ This very popular traditional route follows the right-side crack of the two parallel cracks and gains the cliff's top over four fun pitches. The route protects well with a standard rack. To descend, scramble to the cliff's top and the Misery Ridge Trail. Hike to the right into the gully, and follow Misery Ridge Trail to the cliff's base. **Pitch 1:** (5.6) Start 3 feet to the right of *Peking,* and climb a jumbled dihedral for 20 feet to a chockstone ledge. Move to the left-side crack, and continue up easy rock another 50 feet to a good belay ledge shared with *Peking.* **Pitch 2:** (5.6) Traverse up and right to a steep crack in a dihedral, and climb the crack for 15 feet to the ramp-face above. Maneuver the crack and the ramp-face to a belay ledge. **Pitch 3:** (5.6) Climb the right-side crack up the ramp-face and belay just below the cliff's top. **Pitch 4:** (4th class) Scramble easy rock to the cliff's top.

133. Breakdown In Paradise (5.10b) ★★★ This fun sport route sends the unique pocketed face to the right of *Moscow.* Smear up sloping holds to the first bolt, and climb the fun pocketed face on solid holds past three bolts to the bulging technical crux. Balance through on thin holds, then climb large edges to the top anchors. The bolts are spaced very close, making this a popular line.

North Point

North Point is the most accessible climbing area within the park, with its approach from the viewpoint turnaround parking area taking less than five minutes. Most routes protect very well but can also easily be toproped. Because of this and the easy access, the area is very popular with climbers recently introduced to the sport. Route grades range from easy 5.5 to strenuous 5.13. The area is separated into two main sections, the West Side and the East Side, and the two sides are separated by a 3rd-class-scramble access chimney used by many climbers to travel between the cliff's top and bottom. From the parking area, hike an obvious trail north toward the canyon rim. After about 200 yards, one comes to a distinct fork in the trail. The left trail leads to the base of the rimrock and the far right side of the West Side. Continuing straight brings one to the 3rd-class access chimney. This is the most direct path to access North Point's East Side.

North Point—West Side

The West Side is primarily set aside as a traditional climbing area and is easily accessed via the hiking trail or the 3rd-class chimney. Routes are shown from right to left.

134. Pumpkin Patch (5.5) ✶✶ This short traditional-style route makes a great lead for learning to place gear. Climb large positive holds up the ramp-face to the steep section at the cliff's top, then make a short sequence through the crux to the top anchors. The route protects well with a standard rack.

135. Sweet Spot (5.10c) ✶ Five feet left of *Pumpkin Patch,* an angled overhanging crack rises above a small ceiling. Boulder to the top of a large block, and surmount the triangle-shaped boulder below the small ceiling. Jam the powerful crack to the cliff's top. The

awkward crux lies just above the small ceiling. The route protects well with smaller traditional gear.

136. Handyman (5.7) ✶✶✶ This fun route sends the high-quality crack in the shallow dihedral. It protects well with a standard rack. Scramble up easy rock for 10 feet, then jam and stem the crack and face holds to the top anchors. The crux comes at the route's top.

137. Grandma's House (5.10b) ✶✶ This route's bolts were recently removed, making it a toprope only. On small but positive holds, power over the bulge 3 feet left of *Handyman.* Turn left, then send the short but steep wall while following the hairline seam. Stem the steep rock to the cliff's top. There are two 5.10a cruxes, including the starting bulge and the tricky top-section.

138. Pinch Me (5.11b) ★★★ This route lies 50 feet left of *Grandma's House.* Follow the short trail around the boulder pile to its northeast side. The pumpy sport route pulls through a series of overhangs. Scramble up the easy ramp a few feet to the base of a large, blank overhanging face. Smear the blank wall, and power through on mediocre holds to a resting ledge halfway up. The crux comes between the first and second bolts.

139. Swan Song (5.10b) ★★★ This exciting traditional route climbs through an airy bulge halfway up the cliff. Make an unprotected scramble for 15 feet to a large ledge. Jam through the overhanging crux to great holds made by wedged blocks, then climb easy rock to the cliff's top. The route protects well with 1- to 3-inch cams.

Adam leading *Swan Song*.

140. Sartin R&B (5.10a) ✭✭✭ Thirty feet left of *Swan Song* lies a large deep chimney. This well-protected sport route follows the steep arête on the chimney's left side. The crux comes at the route's steep middle section. Climb the seam and face past the first bolt to an angled ledge. Leverage the face holds, and climb the steep arête to a seam and then the cliff's top.

141. Meat Grinder (5.8) ✭ This traditional route follows the large crack to the left of *Sartin R&B*. Traverse the angled crack up and left to a sloping ledge, then climb face holds and jam the wide crack to the cliff's top. The crux comes through the overhanging bulge halfway up the route, which requires large traditional gear to protect.

142. Thumper (5.8) ✭✭✭ A wonderful hand-size seam zigzags to the cliff's top. Lieback an overhanging crack to a small ledge. Step left, then jam and stem the over-hanging face to the route's top. The route protects well with a standard rack. The pumpy crux comes through the overhanging section at midroute.

143. Little Wonder (5.10b) ✭✭ Climb the little seam just left of the small ceiling 6 feet off the ground, then scramble 10 feet to a small ledge. Jam the fingertip crack while stemming the overhanging rock. The crux comes below the flare at midroute. The route protects well with small traditional gear. Some climbers have difficulty maintaining the power to protect the fingertip crux.

144. Lean Cuisine (5.6) ✭✭ This fun, easy route is ideal for learning to place traditional protection on the lead, and it protects well with a standard rack. The route sends the jumbled corner 5 feet left of *Little Wonder.* Scramble up the easy ramp for 10 feet, and climb the jumbled crack for 15 feet to a small ceiling. Pull over the crux ceiling, then climb the easier rock to the cliff's top. *Lean Cuisine* lies 30 feet right of the 3rd-class scramble used to transcend the cliff's top and bottom.

145. Jersey Shore (5.7) ✭✭ A section of jumbled rock leads to a set of parallel cracks toward the cliff's top. This short traditional route is the farthest left on North Point's west side and lies 20 feet right of the 3rd-class access chimney. The route protects well with traditional gear but is primarily set up as a toprope. The 5.7 crux comes at the final move while pulling over the cliff's top.

North Point—East Side

The East Side's cliff is both taller and steeper than the West Side's. It hosts a greater concentration of more difficult routes, making it suitable for intermediate and expert climbers. In addition to traditional-style leads, the East Side hosts several high-quality sport routes. Approach the East Side via the 3rd-class access chimney. From the base of the access scramble, the first route lies 150 feet to the east, past the large leaning snag. Routes are listed from right to left.

146. Playing With Fire (5.7) ✶✶ The first of three tightly spaced routes on the jumbled wall left of the leaning snag, this traditional route protects well with a standard rack but requires a few oversize pieces to protect the top. Scramble up easy rock for 15 feet to a large ledge and overhanging seam. Pull through the V-shaped seam, then jam past the ceiling to a larger off-width crack. Thrash up the short off-width to the cliff's top, where the crux lies above the small ceiling toward the top.

147. Burn Baby Burn (5.10a) ✶✶✶ This traditional route shares the same start with *Playing With Fire* but then turns left after 15 feet. Scramble easy rock to a hole at midroute. A series of powerful jams and stems pulls one through the overhanging crux to the easier crack above. The route protects well with a standard rack.

148. Firestarter (5.10d) ✶✶ This route tackles the overhang and significant ceiling 3 feet left of *Burn Baby Burn*. Scramble easy rock on great holds to the crux ceiling. Undercling the strenuous ceiling, then power through using a sequence of jams and face holds. Climb the steep rock to the cliff's top. The route protects well with a standard rack.

149. Runaway Bunny (5.11d) ★★ This toprope sends the difficult fingertip seams just right of the large ceiling that lies 20 feet left of *Firestarter*. Paste the smooth rock for 10 feet to the overhanging seams in the shallow corner. Make a short and difficult series of fingertip jams and blank smears through the crux to the better holds just right of the ceiling. Follow a series of long lock-offs on mediocre face holds to a large ledge left of the prominent crack line, then step left and join *If I Ran the Circus* to the cliff's top.

150. If I Ran the Circus (5.10b) ★★★ Start in the shallow corner directly under the large ceiling. Lieback the flake crack to the ceiling and traverse right. The crux comes as you pull over the ceiling's right side to the angled bulge above. Climb easier rock to the cliff's top. The route protects well with traditional gear. Adequately protecting the ceiling can create substantial rope drag on the lead; consequently, the route is usually toproped.

151. Woman In the Meadow (5.11a) ★★★
This wonderful sport route is an area classic.
The constant grade adequately burns the
arms, making the clip into the top anchors a
nervous moment for many climbers. Pull
over the initial bulge on a series of fun holds,
and follow the seam past a series of bolts to a
small triangle-shaped ceiling. Toeing the small
pocket can be helpful. Pull the overhang to
the balancy crux just above the final bolt.

152. The Heathen (5.13a) ★★★ A powerful
line of bolts tackles the desperate ceiling
toward the cliff's top. The first bolt is 15 feet
off the ground, but the sequence is not too
difficult. Most climbers use a clip-stick to mitigate ground-fall potential. Climb a balancy
series of holds to the overhang above, then
tread lightly through the overhang to the crux
ceiling at the last bolt. Heel hook and undercling the tweaky ceiling to the top anchors.

153. Billy Goat (5.11+ ?) ★★★ A splendid wall of high-quality sport routes lies 70 feet left of *The Heathen*. This is the rightmost route. Start on the left side of a featureless block, and use the crack and miniature face holds to climb past the first bolt. At the second bolt, work up and right onto a ramp-face. The desperate crux comes at the second bolt while sequencing over tiny edges onto the ramp-face. Many climbers have pieced the route together, but few pull off the entire sequence. The difficulty eases past the third bolt.

154. Hang It Loose (5.10b) ★★★ Just left of *Billy Goat*, a crack sends the right side of a prominent ceiling. The addition of bolts above the ceiling has negated the original R rating. Climb the easy jumbled crack to the large ceiling, where a series of fun holds pulls one over the top. Above the ceiling, tackle the reachy flat crux past two bolts, then climb easier rock to the cliff's top.

155. Perfect Move (5.10c) ✶✶✶ This high-quality line starts on the left side of the slab below the prominent overhang. Climb fun flake and face holds past two bolts to the small ceiling. Undercling and make a long reach to a sloping ledge above the ceiling, then dyno off the ledge to better holds above. The crux comes between the third and fourth bolts.

156. Headstone (5.9) ✶✶ This toprope starts 3 feet left of *Perfect Move*. Start by surmounting a 3-foot-tall headstone-shaped block, then follow a seam to the right side of a small bulge. Toward the bulge's top, step left to a seam in a shallow open book. Climb steep rock on good holds for 15 feet to a series of easy, dirty ledges leading to the top anchors. The crux comes 15 feet up as one moves high enough to step left of the small bulge.

157. Inspector Fuzz (5.10c/d) ✶✶ Follow a line of closely spaced bolts up a nondescript wall to a small overhang. Start to the right of the first bolt, and make a balancy reach up and left to a mediocre hold above the second bolt. This balancy crux at the second bolt requires precision footwork and body positioning. Follow a series of good holds up steep rock to a small bulge toward the cliff's top, then pull over the bulge's left side to the top anchors.

158. Jungle Fever (5.11b/c) ✶✶✶ This strenuous sport route lies 15 feet left of *Inspector Fuzz*. Climb the 5.10- pillar on small ledges to its top, then continue up the pumpy overhanging face past three bolts to a 2-foot ceiling. Make a long, powerful lock-off to solid holds left of the fifth bolt, and scramble up easy rock to the top-chains.

159. Torrid Zone (5.12a) ✶✶✶ An area classic, the *Torrid Zone* sends perfect rock through a distinct set of features. Work through a series of good holds to a large hole in the rock. Undercling and make a series of precision pinches to better holds at the fourth bolt. Reach to the solid ledges above, and climb easier rock to the top-chains.

THE STEEPLE

Rock Type	Volcanic
Quality of Rock (0–5)	1
Maximum Height	160 feet
Ownership	USFS

■ OVERVIEW

The Steeple is a 160-foot-tall volcanic pinnacle. It has one adventure-lead route and one toprope. The climbing level is best suited for intermediate to expert climbers. The protection can be difficult to place. It takes a full day to climb both routes, which grade 5.7 and 5.11c. The area is undeveloped, and there is not a real trail leading to the rock. The area is open, however, so trails are not necessary. There are only a few bolts on the entire rock. It is too cold to climb here during the winter. The rock is loose, sharp, and chossy, with only a few solid cracks and ledges, but *Killer Bee Cracks* has some solid sections. Rockfall is a major problem and *Killer Bee Cracks* has a few hornet nests on it, so take

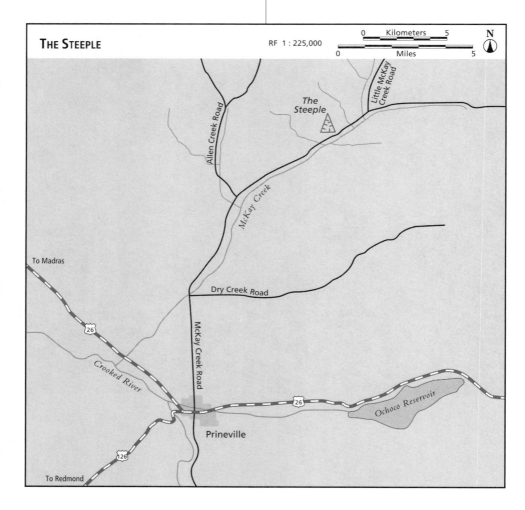

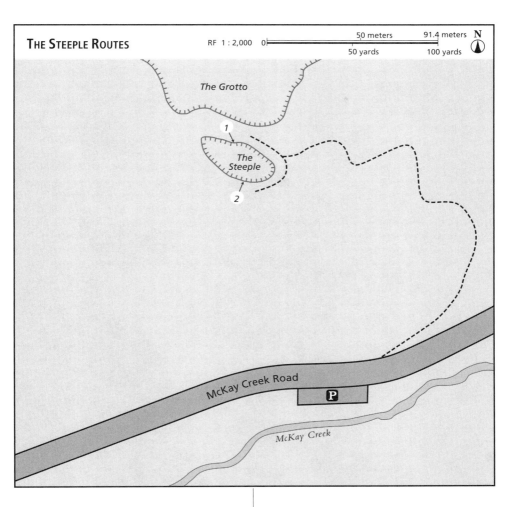

RF 1 : 2,000

50 meters 91.4 meters **N**
50 yards   100 yards

The Grotto

1

The
Steeple

2

McKay Creek Road

P

McKay Creek

the necessary precautions. Free camping is available along the various roads to the north, but you won't find any drinking water or restrooms.

Finding the crags: Halfway through Prineville on U.S. Highway 26, turn north onto North Main Street, which turns into McKay Creek Road. Follow McKay Creek exactly 12.5 miles. The pinnacle is 120 yards up the hill, on the northwest side of the road, about 0.25 mile past the U.S. Forest Service boundary sign. Park along the road, next to the creek. The hike is short but steep.

It's not called the Steeple for nothing.

The Steeple

Both routes are fairly good, but *The Airy Traverse* is an adventure that requires many different techniques. It is definitely not sport climbing. The rockfall can be very dangerous; wear a helmet and take all necessary precautions.

1. The Airy Traverse (5.7 R) ✷ This two-pitch climb is the best way to reach the pinnacle's summit. The route covers many sections of loose rock and protection is poor, but the summit offers such spectacular views, it's worthwhile if done safely. A hammer and pins may be useful for placing protection, and a standard rack is required. **Pitch 1:**

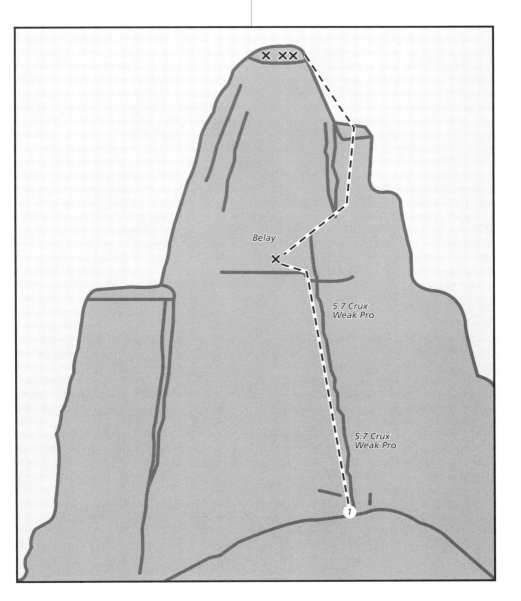

Belay

5.7 Crux
Weak Pro

5.7 Crux
Weak Pro

(5.7) The route starts at the highest point in the notch between the Steeple and the Grotto. Climb the slightly angled crack for 50 feet, then traverse up and left another 10 feet to a belay ledge at the top of pitch 1. There is a single bolt in place at the belay. The crux starts about 10 feet off the ground and continues at solid 5.7 for 20 feet. The crack is thin and dirty, and protection is weak throughout this section. The next 20 feet protects well, and the climbing is easy. Fifty feet up there is a slight over-hang and another 5.7 section where the protection becomes fairly difficult to place. **Pitch 2:** (5.4) Move up and right for 15 feet from the belay ledge. Watch out for loose rock, and keep the belayer out of the way. Climb a nearly vertical flake/crack section for 10 feet, and surmount a block on the west ridge. Protection is very poor through this first 25 feet, but is abundant past this point. Climb another 15 feet of easy rock, from the block to the summit. Three bolts are in place on the summit from which to rappel.

2. Killer Bee Cracks (5.11c) ★★ This is a good, tall toprope. The toprope can be set up with two 50-meter ropes once the summit is reached via *The Airy Traverse*. There are two loose sections, but the rock is solid and clean for the most part. There are also hornet nests hidden behind the flakes. The crux is at the obvious, huge ceiling 15 feet off the ground; the rock is great through this section. The route is pumpy and relentless, and the first good break is 35 feet up. Once through the ceiling, face and crack climb another 30 feet to a solid crack and ramp.

Climb the 5.6 ramp for 40 feet, then tackle a second ceiling. Once through, climb a strenuous, overhanging face up and slightly left for 25 feet to the pillar's middle. From here, climb big ledges and crumbly rock 40 feet to the summit. Two 50-meter ropes can be used to set up this toprope, but they do not offer a lot of room for error. Be careful when rappelling off, or use two 60-meter ropes.

THE BADLANDS

Rock Type	Basalt
Quality of Rock (0–5)	4
Maximum Height	25 feet
Ownership	BLM

■ O V E R V I E W

The Badlands provides bouldering, short topropes, and traditional leads. There are no bolts on the cliff. The climbing level ranges from beginner to intermediate, and most climbs grade between 5.4 and 5.10. The area provides several days of climbing, which is best from fall through spring; summer is hot. The rock is smooth yet sticky, and contains pockets, edges, and cracks. The cliff's top is commonly loose, and the climate is arid; take the necessary precautions. Road 4 is rough and rocky, so a high-clearance vehicle is recommended. During winter months, Road 4 is closed to motorized vehicles north of the junction with Road 8. Camping is available throughout the area, but drinking water and restrooms are not.

Finding the crags: Drive east from Bend on U.S. Highway 20 for 18 miles. After mile marker 17, turn north onto a paved road; a gravel pit lies on the east side. Drive 1 mile and turn left onto the first dirt road, Road 4. At this turnoff there is a billboard containing maps and information. Read the information and take a map if necessary. Drive 2.5 miles to the Badlands Rock, a tall, low-angle dome on the west side of the road. Continue on Road 4 for less than 1 mile to the Drive-In, a lava chasm on the north side of the road. A dirt road leads into it. The South Wall is located 200 yards due south of the Drive-In.

Park in the turnout on the south side of the road, and hike 200 yards due south over an obvious hill covering the skyline.

The Badlands Rock

The Badlands Rock has only a few good climbs. The trails are covered with 5-foot-tall sage, so hiking can be difficult. It is typically more windy here than at the other areas. The following routes are not illustrated.

1. Unknown (5.6) ★★ Start to the right of the overhang, and climb the 25-foot-tall wall of solid rock. The route is covered with positive pockets and ledges.

2. Unknown (5.6) ★ This route is mossy and has bad-fall potential. Climb the left buttress to the wall's top.

3. Unknown (5.6) ★ This route is best identified by the ¼-inch seam, 20 feet up. It lies between the two sage bushes. To gain the cliff's top, climb past the right side of the tallest block. This route has mossy rock and bad-fall potential.

4. Unknown (5.8) ★ Climb the rock's overhanging east face. A toprope is recommended. Bad-fall potential exists.

5. Unknown (5.7) ★ Climb the southwest face on the right side of the arête. A toprope is recommended. Bad-fall potential exists.

6. Unknown (5.9) ★ Climb the southwest face on the left side of the arête. A toprope is recommended. Bad-fall potential exists.

7. Unknown (5.8) ★ Climb the 3-inch crack splitting the block's top. It lies left of the 8-inch crack.

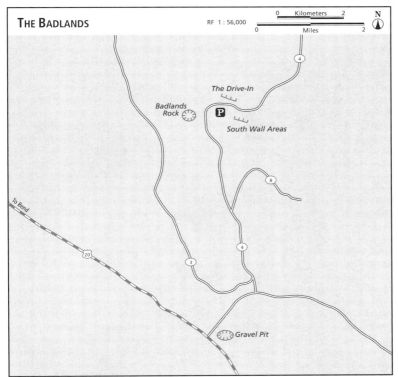

THE BADLANDS

RF 1 : 56,000

Kilometers

Miles

N

The Drive-In

Badlands Rock

P

South Wall Areas

To Bend

20

3

4

8

4

Gravel Pit

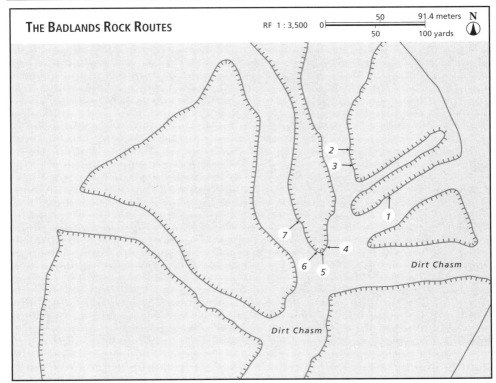

THE BADLANDS ROCK ROUTES

RF 1 : 3,500

91.4 meters

100 yards

N

2

3

1

7

4

6

5

Dirt Chasm

Dirt Chasm

Michael feeling right at home in the Badlands.

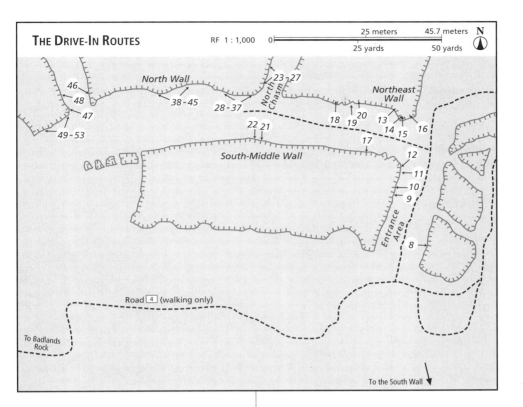

RF 1 : 1,000   0

25 meters   45.7 meters   **N**

25 yards   50 yards

46

48

47

49 - 53

North Wall

38 - 45

28 - 37

North Chasm

23 - 27

22 21

17

South-Middle Wall

18 19 20

13

14 15

16

12

11

10

9

Entrance Area

8

Northeast Wall

Road 4 (walking only)

To Badlands
Rock

To the South Wall

The Drive-In

The Drive-In provides excellent routes on solid rock. Parking is found within 20 feet of the routes. The dirt is soft and cushions landings when bouldering.

The Drive-In—Entrance Area

8. Lean Pockets (5.10b) ✶✶✶ Not pictured. This route is an area classic. Start under the first overhang, 20 feet in from the wall's end, left of the bushes near the top of the cliff. The pocketed crux requires lots of power.

9. Kindergarten (5.4) ✶✶✶ This area classic is an easy route. The overhanging start is entertaining.

10. Unknown (5.4) ✶✶ This ramp makes a good climb.

11. Willies (5.7) ✶✶ The crux lies toward the top of the cliff. This route gives many climbers "the willies."

12. Unknown (5.5) ✶✶ This boulder problem is the best 5.5 at the Badlands. It is relatively tall.

13. Unknown (5.8) ✶ Not pictured. Climb the broken crack on the west side of wall C. It lies 3 feet in from the right-side arête. The moves are awkward.

The Drive-In—Northeast Wall

14. The Needle (5.9) ✶✶ Climb the bulging arête. This route is enjoyable and pumps up one's forearms.

15. Hot Pockets (5.6) ✶✶ This route is a good 5.6. Because of the height of the cliff, a toprope is recommended.

16. Varassic (5.5) ✶✶ This line makes a good lead or highball problem.

17. Unknown (5.7) ✶✶ Not pictured. Climb the ½-inch crack between the two bulges for 10 feet. Finish by climbing 3 feet of face with positive holds. The route lies on the first solid wall on the left as one enters the back portion of the Drive-In.

18. Unknown (5.9) ✶✶ Not pictured. Routes 18 through 20 surround the tall, solid ramp on the cliff. Climb the inside face on the wall left of *Chucky Cheese*.

19. Chucky Cheese (5.3) ✶✶ Not pictured. Climb the middle ramp, and exit left of the top's ceiling. This route is the best 5.3 at the Badlands.

20. Unknown (5.6) ✶ Not pictured. On the wall right of *Chucky Cheese,* climb the face to the right of the bulging arête. The middle section contains loose rock.

The Drive-In—
South-Middle Wall

21. Good-N-Plenty (5.8) ★★ Climb pockets and jugs to the cliff's top.

22. Unknown (5.7) ★★ Climb the solid crack and face.

The Drive-In—North Chasm

23. Dirty Snacks (5.7) ★★★ This route is a classic highball–boulder problem.

24. Unknown (5.6) ★★ Climb the cliff to the right of the jugs and holes.

25. Unknown (5.6) ★ This is a straightforward, easy boulder problem.

26. Pewees Revenge (5.8) ★★★ This is a great boulder problem. Climb out of the left side of the cave using great holds.

27. Unknown (5.6) This route is short and is not recommended.

The Drive-In—North Wall

28. Unknown (5.7) ★★ This route has solid ledges and pockets.

29. Unknown (5.8) ★★ This steep problem is commonly enjoyed.

30. Stairmaster 2000 (5.6) ★★ Climb the easy ramp using solid ledges.

31. Airborn (5.9) ★★ This is a fun open book with a pushy crux.

32. Unknown (5.8) ★★ Climb the easy ramp, then tackle the interesting crux.

33. Hit This (5.8) ★★ Climb the exciting arête.

34. Unknown (5.4) This route climbs the easy, fat crack.

35. Unknown (5.5) Broken glass lies near the cliff's top. This route is not recommended.

36. Unknown (5.7) ★ Climb the wall, then exit to the right to avoid the tree.

37. Pockets-O-Gold (5.8) ★★★ Climb the solid pockets up the tall wall. The exciting crux comes about halfway up. This is an area classic.

38. Area 51 (5.8) ✻ The moss on top of the roof diminishes the quality of this route.

39. Cyclops (5.8) ✻✻✻ Start directly below the small ceiling. Use good holds to surmount the cliff's top.

40. Unknown (5.6) ✻ Climb the easy ramp to the cliff's top.

41. Unknown (5.3) This route is very easy.

42. Unknown (5.6) ✻ Climb the wall to the right of the small cave.

43. Unknown (5.7) ✻✻ This route is a variation to *Y-Not*. It is tall and enjoyable.

44. Y-Not (5.7) ✻✻ This is a good route that climbs solid, clean rock.

45. Unknown (5.6) ✻ Climb the easy arête.

46. AWOL (5.7) ✻✻ Not pictured. This route lies to the left of the deep, see-through gully. The start is mossy, and the bulging crux near the top is exciting.

The Drive-In—West End

47. Eightball (5.4) ★★ This tall route is easy but enjoyable. Watch for loose rock near the top.

48. Carnival (5.7) ★★★ Climb the jugs out of the cave. The airy finish is exciting. This route is highly recommended.

49. Unknown (5.4) Climb the short, low-angle slab.

50. Unknown (5.4) Climb the easy ramp. The top is loose.

51. Unknown (5.5) ★ This is a decent problem but is short.

52. Unknown (5.6) ★ The cave start is exciting. Great holds make the route easy.

53. Foot Jam (5.6) ★★ Climb the tall crack splitting the ramp. The exciting crux comes near the top.

The South Wall

The South Wall provides great climbing. In general, it is steeper than the Drive-In. The area has several good 5.10s. No man-made trails lead to the South Wall. It is common to lose one's direction; take the necessary precautions.

The South Wall— Northwest Wall

54. Drag a Day (5.7) ★★ Climb the solid crack.

55. Hard One (5.10a) ★★★ This arête has great holds. The route is an area classic.

56. Pocket Protector (5.6) ★★★ Climb and stem the crack and great face holds. The crack protects well with traditional gear.

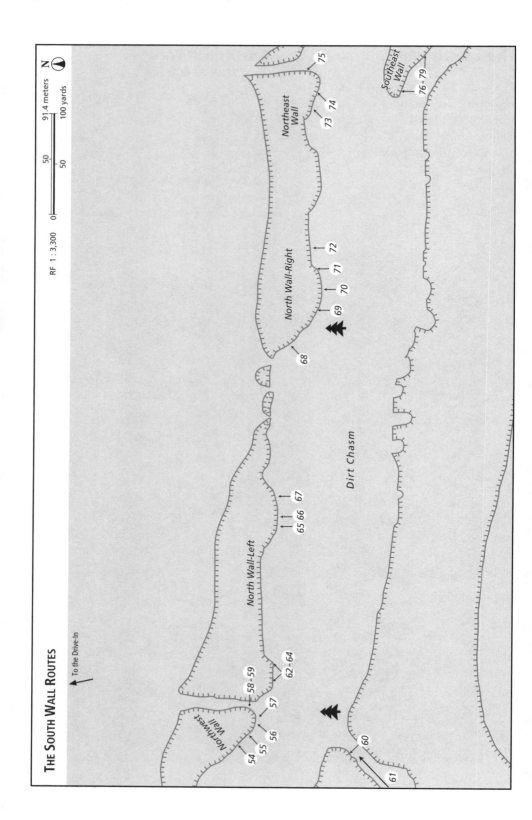

THE SOUTH WALL ROUTES

To the Drive-In

RF 1 : 3,300

N

0   50   91.4 meters
0   50   100 yards

Northwest Wall

54
55
56
57

58-59

62-64

65 66 67

North Wall-Left

Dirt Chasm

60

61

68

69 70 71 72

North Wall-Right

73 74

75

Northeast Wall

76-79

Southeast Wall

57. Stealers (5.7) ★★★ This is a great line that tests the nerves of most climbers. Huge jugs keep the grade down.

58. Unknown (5.7) ★★ Climb the nice crack.

59. Unknown (5.8) ★★ Move around the bulge using the huge pockets.

60. Unknown (5.7) ★ Not pictured. Climb the pocketed wall split by a thin seam. It lies 10 feet in from the corner of the cliff.

61. Omega Traverse (5.7) ★★★ Not pictured. Traverse the whole west wall up the hill. This is a long traverse that tests one's endurance.

The South Wall—North Wall

62. Power House (5.10a) ★★★ Use power to gain the overhang. This route is enjoyable.

63. Unknown (5.10c) ★★ This route has a good finish. The crack is sharp and is painful to jam.

64. Unknown (5.9) ★★ This is a nice, enjoyable line. Be cautious around the loose flake.

65. Captain Jack (5.9) ✶✶ This route climbs one of the tallest walls at the Badlands.

66. Unknown (5.6) ✶✶ Climb the tall face following the ¾-inch crack.

67. Unknown (5.6) ✶✶ Climb up good holds, then step right to finish.

68. Unknown (5.7) ✶ Not pictured. This route lies west of the tree. Climb the bulging buttress west of the ceiling.

69. Unknown (5.6) This route is not very tall. Climb to the right of the crack.

70. Unknown (5.5) ✫ Move up easy holds to the cliff's top.

71. Silver Shield (5.7) ✫✫ This boulder problem follows a line of clean, steep rock up the wall.

72. Big Bleed (5.7) ✫✫ This route has great moves. The bottom lacks good footholds.

The South Wall—
Northeast Wall

73. Standoff Pillar (5.7) ✰✰ Climb up the detached pillar. This is an enjoyable climb.

74. Unknown (5.8) ✰✰ Climb the steep face to the cliff's top.

75. Unknown (5.8) ✰ The pushy crux comes toward the top of this exciting route. There is a strong potential for a bad fall, so be cautious.

The South Wall—
Southeast Wall

76. Unknown (5.7) ✶ Climb the wall to the right side of the large crack.

77. Unknown (5.7) ✶ Climb the pockets to send this short wall.

78. Unknown (5.7) ✶ Climb the short, solid face.

79. Unknown (5.7) This problem is very short and is not recommended.

MEADOW PICNIC AREA

Rock Type	Volcanic Tuff
Quality of Rock (0–5)	5
Maximum Height	35 feet
Ownership	USFS

■ OVERVIEW

Meadow Picnic Area provides great crack climbing, topropes, and bouldering. Traditional gear and several 10-foot lengths of webbing are necessary for setting up topropes. Some climbs have toprope anchors in place. The climbing level ranges from intermediate to expert, and it takes a week to climb all of the routes in one's grade. Most routes grade 5.9 and up, with only a few good ones easier than 5.9. The rock is solid

and clean. The weather for climbing is best from spring through fall; winters are cold and there is often snow. Ticks become abundant during the spring, and there are scorpions in the area as well. Take the necessary precautions. Strict climbing regulations for the area are posted on a sign at the river trailhead. Please read and obey these regulations. Free camping is available on most nearby dirt roads spurring from the highway. Drinking water and restrooms are not available.

Finding the crags: From Bend, drive west on Century Drive toward Mount Bachelor for approximately 3 miles. Before mile marker 6, turn south to Meadow Picnic Area. The road is next to Widgi Creek Golf Course. Drive less than 1 mile, and park in the first parking area. Hike east to the river trail and the climbing information sign, and follow the river trail to one of several cliff-access trails.

Ben loving life at the Meadow Picnic Area.

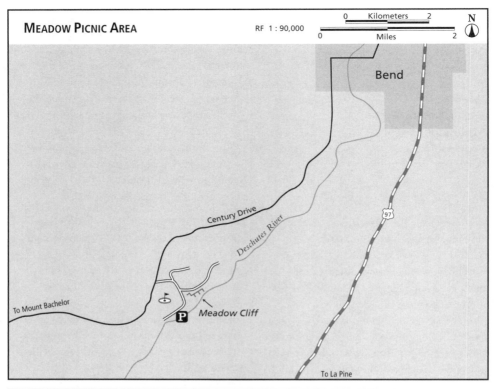

MEADOW PICNIC AREA

RF 1 : 90,000

0 — Kilometers — 2
0 — Miles — 2

N

Bend

Century Drive

Deschutes River

97

To Mount Bachelor

P

Meadow Cliff

To La Pine

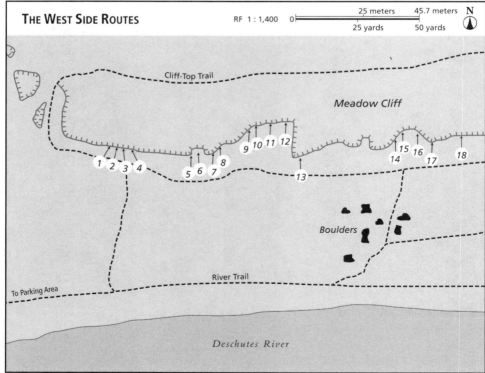

THE WEST SIDE ROUTES

RF 1 : 1,400

0 — 25 meters — 45.7 meters
0 — 25 yards — 50 yards

N

Cliff-Top Trail

Meadow Cliff

9 10 11 12

1 2 3 4

5 6 7 8

13

15 16

14

17

18

Boulders

River Trail

To Parking Area

Deschutes River

Rock climbing, white-water rafting, and golf all in the same place—the only thing better would be great crack climbing, topropes, and bouldering in the same place.

The West Side

1. The Shining (5.11a) ✽✽✽ This is a great face climb. Most climbers start left to avoid the 5.13 lower crux. The top crux grades 5.11a and requires balancing up little pockets and pumpy edges. Toprope anchors are in place.

2. Chinese Sun (5.9) ✽✽ Fun little pockets guide you through the balancy 5.9 section. The bolts on top of the route do not have hangers. Use nuts and back up the belay on nearby bolts.

3. Wide Jam (5.10a) ✽ This is a difficult crack climb. The crux comes through the route's lower midsection. The face pushes one outward. The crack is somewhat dirty and sharp, so be careful. Traditional gear is necessary to set up a toprope.

4. Unconscious Contingency (5.11c) ✽✽ This route is relatively easy except for the blank section under the overhang. One must move through this crux's tiny edges, traversing left from the good pockets to the arête. The overhang pushes climbers out, though it offers great moves. Two bolts are in place on top.

5. Jesus Saves (5.11a) ✭✭✭ This is a difficult but awesome right-facing arête. The crux comes at the ledge halfway up. There is only one bolt at the top, and it does not have a hanger. Traditional gear is necessary to set up a toprope.

6. Crescent Crack (5.10b) ✭ The crux lies at the route's top. Through this section the crack is wide and steep; this is a good off-width crack. There is one bolt without a hanger on top.

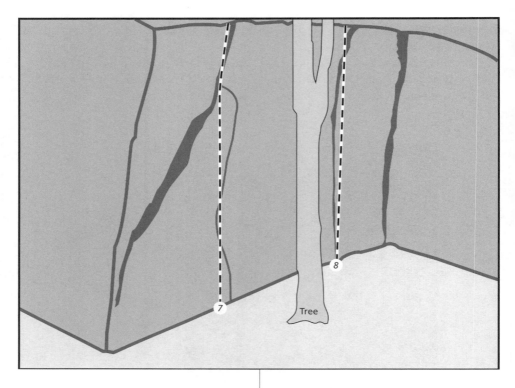

7. Kitzen Coyote (5.8) This crack is dirty and sharp. It is not a very good climb.

8. Straight Split (5.9) ★★ This is a great crack climb and protects very well. The crux comes right off the ground. The wall is very flat.

9. Happy Man (5.10a) ✶✶ The route climbs a perfect dihedral. Lieback the clean 2-inch crack. Two bolts with no hangers are on top.

10. Pre-School (5.6) ✶✶ This route climbs between two cracks. The left crack is about 4 inches wide and protects well with large gear. *Pre-School* is a great beginner route and is one of the few good, easy routes in the area. The face has many big ledges. There are no top anchors.

11. Rad Ramp (5.12a) ✶✶✶ Start on the left side of the face, then climb up and traverse to the middle of the ramp for the finish. This is a great but very difficult ramp,

with tiny ledges and pockets. Two bolts are in place on top.

12. Pure Hand Jam (5.9) ✶✶✶ The crux of the climb comes right off the ground; the top is much easier. Jam the crack to pull over the overhang.. The crack provides solid hand jams. Anchors from the two nearest climbs can be used for setting up a toprope.

13. Moonstone (5.11d) ✶✶✶ This is a much-enjoyed route. The crux comes moving to the left arête and using it to aid through the blank section. Precision footwork is required. Toprope anchors are in place.

14. Tick-Tack (5.10b) This climb is short but strenuous. The crack is dirty and sharp.

15. Pounded Nail (5.6) ✶ Use the wide crack and the face to climb to the pillar's top.

16. The Psycho (5.10c) ✶✶✶ The crack protects well. The top forces one to make a series of strenuous jams to pass the large roof, requiring good strength.

17. Homer's Flake (5.7) ✶ The route follows a fun ramp to a crack, then exits the cliff. The crux comes as you step off the flake.

18. Search for the Stars (5.11b) ★★★ This face is a highly favored toprope. Wonderful, fluid moves over skimpy holds on steep rock make this an area classic.

The Backside

19. Flaky Jake (5.10a) ✯✯ The route climbs a large flake that creates a 6-inch-wide crack. Performing a lieback makes it easy. Two bolts are in place at the top.

20. Cerchunk Crack (5.7) ✯✯ Follow the crack and broken flake to the top. The crux comes as you step right, off the flake and onto the big ledge. There are many good holds. Long runners from nearby bolts can be used to set up a toprope.

21. Maiden in the Meadow (5.12d) ✯ This rock is great, though many find the nearby tree annoying. The route has two difficult parts. The bottom face requires creative pinching and fancy footwork. Once above, move right and climb the arête to the top of the ceiling. Many use a heel hook for the finish. Two bolts are on top.

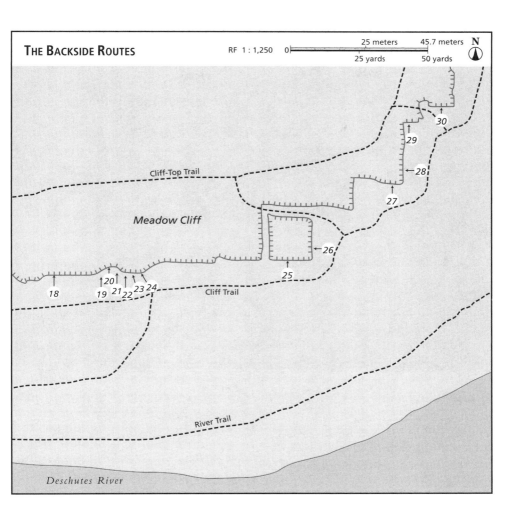

THE BACKSIDE ROUTES

RF 1 : 1,250   0

25 meters   45.7 meters   N

25 yards   50 yards

Cliff-Top Trail

Meadow Cliff

30

29

28

27

26

25

18   19 21 20 23 24
         22

Cliff Trail

River Trail

Deschutes River

22. Black Angel (5.10a) ★★★ This great crack protects well and offers excellent finger jams. The crux comes at the small ceiling two-thirds of the way up. It provides great stemming practice. Two bolts are on top; one has no hanger.

23. Dew, Chalk, and Blood (5.10a) ★★ The sharp crack slightly degrades this pumpy and powerful route. The crux comes at the small overhang. The bolts on top of *Black Angel* can be used to set up a toprope. Traditional gear may be helpful.

24. Solstice (5.9) ★★★ This route is the area classic, and more people climb it than any other. The middle section is difficult to protect. Few climbers lead the route. Two bolts are in place for a toprope.

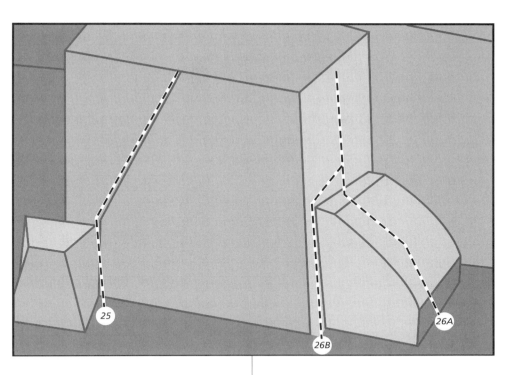

25. Split Block Hallway (5.9) ✰✰ The 5.9 grade assumes one uses the large block at the route's base, as not using it makes the route much more difficult. Most climbers lieback and walk up the slanted crack.

26. Zitty Craters (5.7) ✰ The crux comes near the wall's top. A long lock-off between good holds is required. The route has two starts. **A:** Climb the easy ramp to the east of the wall. **B:** Climb the base of the south wall. Start A is recommended.

27. Hercules (5.12a) ✶✶ This route climbs the 8-inch-wide crack splitting the block's face. The crack makes a good off-width climb. The crux lies at the route's start; small edges inside the crack are useful for ascending this section. The face also has small but useful features.

28. Camino (5.13b) ✶✶ The bouldery start to this relatively short route is extremely difficult. The handholds are small and spread out, and very few footholds exist. Ascending the route requires great strength and balance. A third of the way up, the grade drops to sustained 5.11.

29. Right on Joe (5.10a) ✶✶ This climb ascends a perfect dihedral made by blank walls. The 1½-inch-wide crack produces solid hand jams. Many climbers use a lieback. The crux comes about halfway up. The wall overhangs a little. Traditional gear is needed to set up a toprope.

30. Todo the Wondermut (5.10b) ✭ This face makes a decent route. The technical crux comes at the bottom. Stretchy moves are required to reach a good hold on the right. From here, weave your way through pockets to the top.

LA PINE WALL

Rock Type	Basalt
Quality of Rock (0–5)	2
Maximum Height	55 feet
Ownership	USFS

■ OVERVIEW

La Pine Wall is tucked away in a scenic forest of old-growth pines. The cliff is about one-quarter of a mile long. The rock is good, hard basalt, and some portions are relatively clean. The routes are traditional-style face and crack climbing. Only two bolts reside on the cliff. The cliff-top can be accessed relatively easily for setting up topropes. The climbing level is best suited for intermediate to expert climbers, with route grades ranging from 5.8 to 5.12c. Documented routes can be climbed in two days, though the area has potential for new ones. Climbing is best spring through fall; winters are often too wet and cold. One can camp anywhere in the area. Drinking water and restrooms are unavailable.

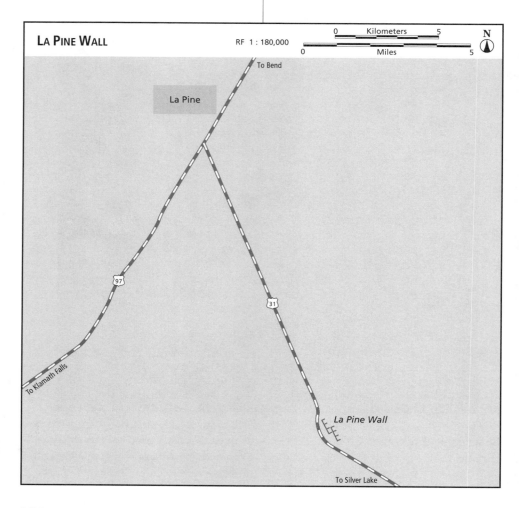

The easy-to-access La Pine Wall spans almost one-quarter mile.

Finding the crags: From La Pine, drive south on U.S. Highway 97 for 1.5 miles and turn southeast onto Highway 31, toward Silver Lake and Lakeview. Turn left (east), 0.5 mile after mile marker 10, onto the first dirt road. The tan and white cliff should be visible several hundred yards up the hill. Drive 0.25 mile to the parking area. Several deer trails lead to the wall; use any combination of these to reach the cliff. Hike east along the cliff until the top can be reached by easy scrambling. Use this approach for setting up topropes.

The first dirt road leading from the highway to the parking area is faint and difficult to see, so it is commonly missed. If this happens, turn onto the next road leading left (east); this road has a stop sign. Follow it a few hundred yards, then take the first road on the left, which leads to the parking area.

La Pine Wall

1. Little Red Stairs (5.8) ★★ This fun route protects well for leading. The top is solid, and protection is abundant for setting up a belay. The crux comes one-quarter of the way up. Pulling over the first bulge is awkward. The rock is solid and clean.

2. Slopers (5.12c) ★★ This face makes a great toprope. The crux comes near the bottom as you traverse up and right. The holds are downward sloping, and good footholds are difficult to find. A fine covering of dust makes the rock slick. The grade would drop significantly if the rock were cleaned. The fluid, difficult moves make this a highly favored route.

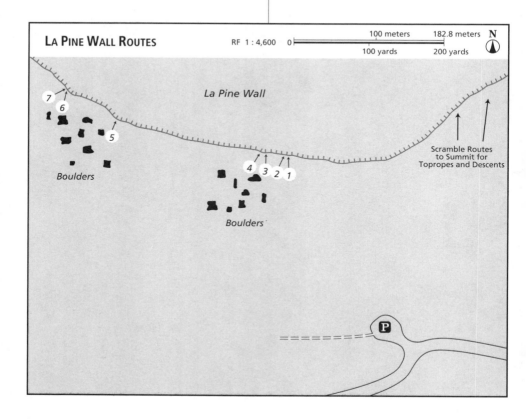

3. Beer Foam (5.10a) ★ Protection on this route is minimal; it should only be toproped. Start to the left, then traverse right across the mossy ledge. This section has good hand-holds. For the rest of the route, the moves and holds are nothing special. The route's top is mossy and is often avoided. Several flakes in the middle of the route are loose; take the necessary precautions.

4. Follow the Brown Crack (5.9) ★★★ This route shares the start with *Beer Foam* and is a highly recommended and enjoyable toprope. The moves are pleasant, and the rock is solid and sticky. Lieback the gray bulge toward the top, then climb up and right for the exit.

5. Double Pump (5.12a) ★ The route's bottom is loose, so be careful. Climb 15 feet to the angled crack splitting the lower block. Starting in the crack is difficult, but the difficulty drops once the initial moves have been made. From the top of the lower block, move up and right. Climb a shallow ramp to the bottom of the second overhanging block. The inside of this crack is dirty, and this section is very difficult. Jam, kick, fight, and stem your way through the huge overhang. Bring large protection for the block's top. Once on top, scramble up and right for 10 feet to a large pyramid-shaped rock, and lasso this rock for the rappel. Two 10-foot lengths of webbing and rappel rings are needed. The route protects well with a standard rack.

6. Skip Tarnagun (5.9) ★★ Start directly under the large ceiling, and use power to surmount the overhanging flake. Climb up and left to the flat wall, then climb the wall a few feet. Traverse left under the ceiling to the flake arête on *Shroom Beetle Carnival;* this section is the crux. The two routes join here, and they share the same set of anchors at the top. The route can be led with traditional gear, but the rope drag becomes very bad. Toproping is recommended.

7. Shroom Beetle Carnival (5.8) ★★ Start under the large block, and scramble up and left to the ramp. Follow the ramp to the flake arête. Climb the flake arête, then scramble to the two-bolt belay. The flake arête makes a fun but scary lead. Traditional gear is necessary for leading the route.

CRACK IN THE GROUND

Rock Type	Basalt
Quality of Rock (0–5)	3
Maximum Height	50 feet
Ownership	BLM

■ OVERVIEW

Crack in the Ground is a narrow chasm splitting the earth's surface for nearly 2 miles. The rock is jumbled basalt and offers traditional-style crack climbing and topropes. The level of climbing ranges from beginner to intermediate, with route grading from 5.5 to 5.10d. The area is well developed, though not specifically for climbing. The road and trail are clearly marked, but there are no bolts or permanent anchors in the area. The rock is solid and edgy; some uncleaned portions are mossy. It takes several days to climb all of the documented routes, and there is potential for many more. Climbing is available year-round, though winters are cold and there is often snow. The crack's deeper portions stay cool all year and hold snow into early summer. There is loose rock on the cliff's top above many of the routes, so some top-belays are difficult to set up. The climate is very arid; take the necessary precautions. Crack in the Ground is a natural scenic area. Limit chalk use, and do not make new trails or place permanent anchors. Free camping is available on any of the nearby roads. Drinking water and restrooms can be found in Christmas Valley.

Finding the crags: From Christmas Valley, turn north onto Crack in the Ground Road and follow it for 8 miles to the Crack in the Ground parking area. There are signs leading to the crack. At the parking area, hike east on the trail for 0.25 mile to the crack's entrance. Turn right and follow the trail southward into the crack.

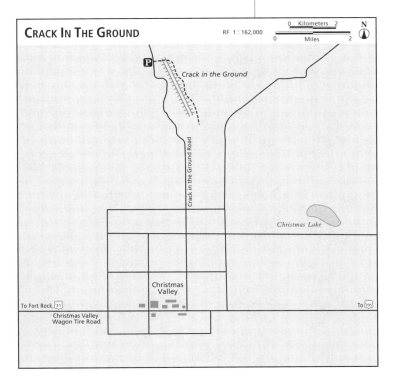

CRACK IN THE GROUND

RF 1 : 162,000

Crack in the Ground

Crack in the Ground Road

Christmas Lake

Christmas Valley

To Fort Rock, 31

To 395

Christmas Valley
Wagon Tire Road

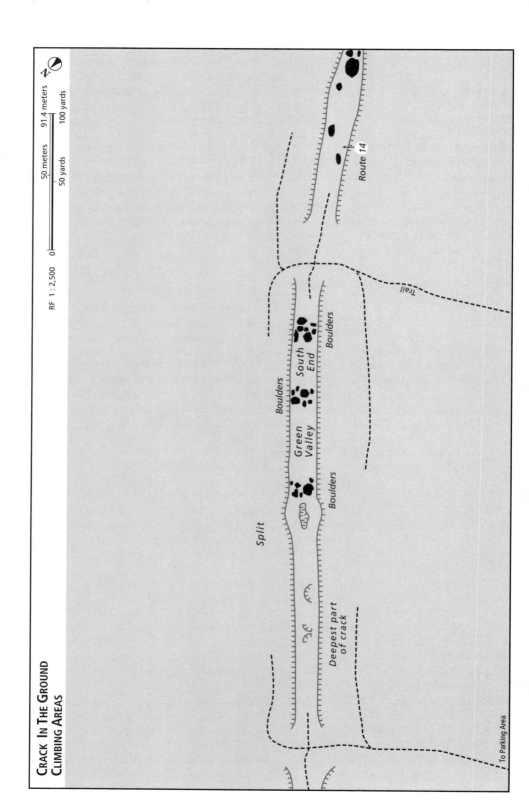

CRACK IN THE GROUND
CLIMBING AREAS

RF 1 : 2,500

50 meters   91.4 meters
0   50 yards   100 yards

N

Split

Deepest part
of crack

Boulders

Green
Valley

Boulders

South
End

Boulders

Trail

Route 14

To Parking Area

This unique climbing experience at Crack in the Ground is well worth the long drive.

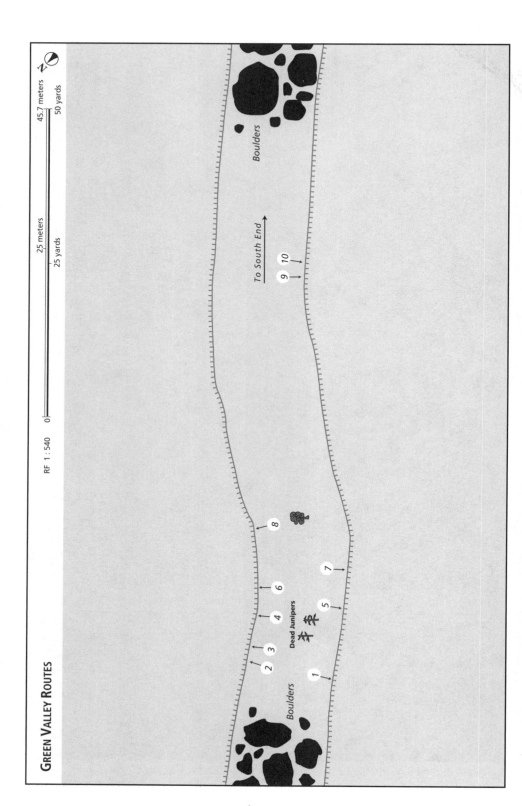

GREEN VALLEY ROUTES

RF 1 : 540

45.7 meters

50 yards

25 meters

25 yards

0

To South End

Boulders

Boulders

Dead Junipers

Green Valley

1. Pan Fry (5.7) ✶ Start 15 feet past the last large boulder and below a red flake and small roof. This route can be led with traditional gear. The bouldery crux comes at the route's start. Climb the crack and large ledges to the flake halfway up, and step left to the plant. Climb up and out the ceiling's left side.

2. Pilsner (5.5) ★★★ Parallel cracks split the wall and make a shallow dihedral. This fun route protects well, climbs clean and solid rock, and is easy to set a top-belay on.

3. Adjustable Ledge (5.9) ★★ The bouldery crux comes at the route's start, which has small ledges and lacks good footholds. Climb good holds through the shallow arête and face to the top. Use the nearby trees for setting a top-belay.

4. Have Faith (5.9) ★★★ This route is good and solid, though some holds are mossy. Climb the steep arête to the top, using holds on both faces. The technical crux comes halfway, when the footholds disappear. Use

the crack on the left- and the right-side arête to climb the steep top, and use the nearby trees for setting up a top-belay.

5. Moonshine (5.8) ★★ This toprope starts a few feet left of the small, almost-dead junipers. Climb the flat, overhanging wall to the crack in the shallow dihedral, then stem and jam the crack to the top. The tricky crux comes toward the top, where there are few good handholds.

6. Smoke-In (5.9) ★★★ This toprope is easy to set up using the trees 50 feet away. Climb the blocky arête to the top, using good holds on both faces. The holds are small through the steep crux at the route's top.

7. Go-Go-Go (5.10c) ★★ This toprope is the next crack left of *Moonshine*. Great holds take one through the overhanging start and finish. The double overhangs pump out many climbers, and the top requires a long lock-off to a mossy ledge.

8. Patchwork (5.7) ★ A thin seam splits the face behind the bush and protects well enough to lead. Use the large ledges right of the seam, then follow it through the open book and crux at the route's top.

9. Happy Dog (5.7) ★★ This toprope starts on the pocketed face next to the deep over-hanging crack. Climb the face and crack to the top and the steep crux, then climb the good holds on the right to exit.

10. Gork (5.10b) ★★★ This route climbs a great and unique pocketed face. Climb the face then outside arête to the top; good pockets on the left face are helpful. The crux comes halfway up. Use the arête to pass the blank face.

South End

11. Cheese Nip (5.10a) ✶✶ This fun, short crack-climb protects well. Stem the blank faces. Climb the crack and face holds through the crux halfway up, and continue to the route's top.

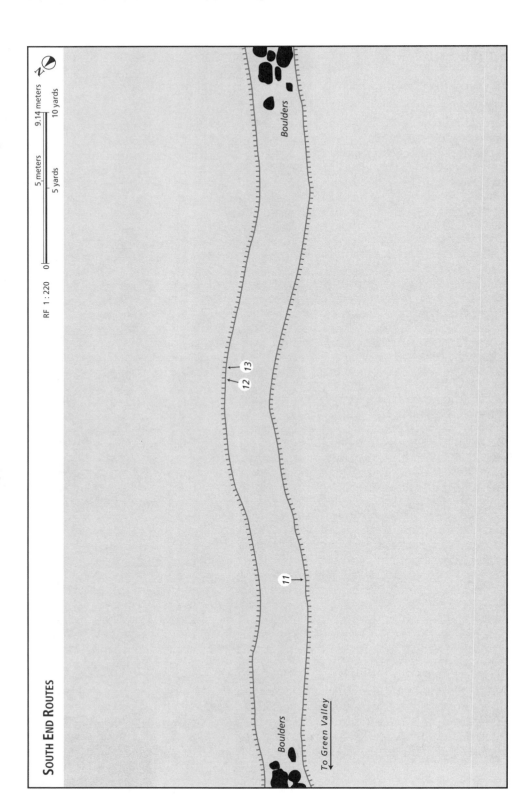

SOUTH END ROUTES

RF 1 : 220

0   5 meters   9.14 meters

5 yards   10 yards

N

Boulders

12
13

11

Boulders

To Green Valley

12. Kidney Beans (5.6) ★ Two wide cracks create a shallow dihedral. This route sends the left-side crack. The bottom is difficult to protect due to the crack's width. Stem, jam, and climb the face holds to the top, which is solid and has great holds.

13. Jumbled Cranium (5.5) ★★ Climb the large crescent-shaped crack on the right side. Use off-width jams and great face holds to climb the solid top.

The Second Crack

Beyond the trail the crack continues for a short while, but a pile of boulders eventually blocks one's exploration. This second crack contains one great route and many other possibilities.

14. McCrackin (5.10d) ✭✭✭ This route lies in the second section of Crack in the Ground, approximately 50 yards into the crack on the west side. Although out of the way, it is a classic and worth the extra walk. This section of solid rock is mostly clean. Climb the overhanging seam in the open book for 15 feet; the crux lies toward the open book's top. Follow the easy crack and face up the dihedral, then continue up the right-side crack to the top. This is a tall and strenuous route with great rock.

YOUTLKUT PILLARS

Rock Type	Andesite
Quality of Rock (0–5)	2
Maximum Height	110 feet
Ownership	USFS

■ OVERVIEW

Youtlkut Pillars has several cracks and faces to climb. Many routes can be led, but require large gear. Climbing is well suited for beginner and intermediate climbers, with all routes grading below 5.10a. The area provides several days of climbing. Trails allow access to the cliff's top and bottom, and pullouts in the vicinity provide parking. Many routes require traditional gear for setting up topropes, but some have top anchors in place. These anchors are set back from the cliff's top. Several longs slings, up to 30 feet, are required for setting up topropes. The area lies just above 4,000 feet, and snow blocks access throughout the winter and spring. The rock is solid but also sharp, and it is common for ropes to get stuck in the cracks. Take the necessary precautions. Youtlkut Pillars is a natural scenic area. Limit chalk use and do not make new trails or place new anchors. One can camp for free anywhere in the area. Pay camping sites with services are available along the river.

Finding the crags: Drive east from Roseburg on Highway 138 for 15 miles to the town of Glide. Just before mile marker 15, turn south onto Little River Road (USFS Road 27), and follow it for 30 miles to the junction with Snowbird Road (USFS Road 2715). Turn left (east) onto Snowbird Road and follow it 2.5 miles to the junction with USFS Road 230. Turn left (north) onto USFS 230 and drive 0.25 mile to the parking area. There are signs to the rock once you reach the junction with USFS Road 230.

Or, from Roseburg, drive east on US 138 for 32 miles and turn south onto Panther Creek Road. Go less than a mile, then turn left onto Calf Ridge Road (USFS Road 4720). Continue 11 miles to a fork in the road and stay left on USFS 4720. Go approximately 2 miles to the junction with Snowbird Road (USFS 2715). Turn left on Snowbird Road, toward Twin Lakes Trail, and follow it for nearly 0.5 mile to USFS Road 230. Turn left and follow signs to Youtlkut Pillars, which lies 0.25 mile down the road. This route can be faster but may also be blocked by debris because of its infrequent use.

YOUTLKUT PILLARS

RF 1 : 131,000

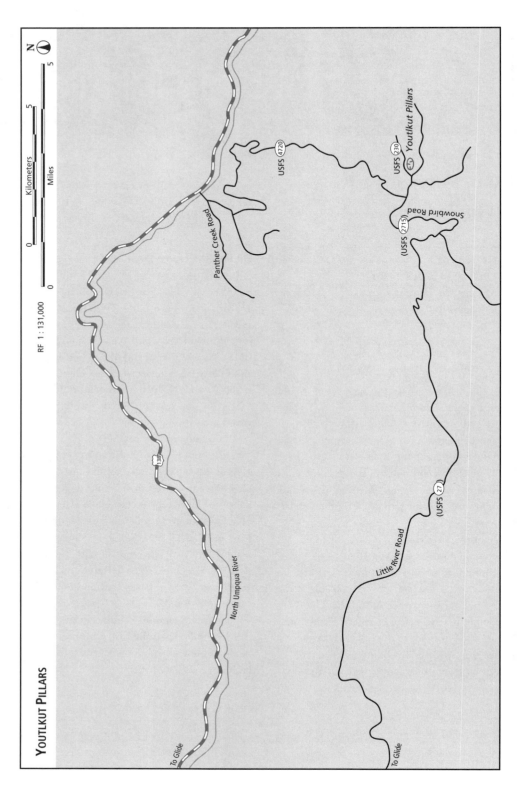

To Glide

North Umpqua River

Panther Creek Road

USFS 4720

USFS 230

Youtlkut Pillars

Snowbird Road

(USFS 2715)

138

Little River Road

(USFS 27)

To Glide

N

Kilometers
0   5

Miles
0   5

These manageable pillars are easier to climb than pronounce.

Youtlkut Pillars

A trail on the left side of the rock provides access to the top and the setting up of topropes. Routes 1, 2, 7, and 8 require traditional gear for setting up topropes; all of the others have fixed protection in place. Placing protection is most convenient up to 20 feet away from the cliff's edge. Use several long runners to reduce rope drag. The cliff height makes two ropes necessary on Routes 7 through 12 if the toprope is not set low enough.

1. Wet N Cold (5.6) This route is mossy and dirty, and would be better if it were cleaned. Because of loose rock, use caution to reach the bottom. The route is fairly sustained. The crux comes about two-thirds of the way up.

2. Genesis (5.10a) This is not a good route. The bottom is mossy, and 25 feet up, above the flake, protection gets difficult to place and is weak. There are two 5.9 cruxes. The first is at the small 6-inch ceiling 35 feet up; the second is at the bulge on top of the route.

3. Alley Oop (5.9) ✶✶ The route protects well with traditional gear. Use the excellent face holds and great cracks to surmount the 50-foot-tall pillar. Once on top, step a few feet right and join *Chinquapin*. The route is fairly sustained, but the technical crux comes toward the top. On top of the 50-foot pillar is a single bolt for directing topropes from *Chinquapin*.

4. Chinquapin (5.6) ✶✶ This route provides a good variety of moves. It protects fairly well but requires large traditional gear. For this reason, it is a better toprope than lead. The crux comes at the last section; the holds are hidden.

5. Chinquapin Right Variation (5.6) ✶✶ This is a nice variation. Start on the pillar's right side, and stem, jam, and use face holds to surmount the 25-foot-tall pillar. Step left and join *Chinquapin*.

6. 3-D (5.7) ✶✶✶ This is the best route on the crag. It is short enough to avoid the sharp rock toward the cliff's top, and it does not require much gear to lead. The rock is solid and clean. Climb the cracks and face to reach the top anchors, which are hiding below the small ceiling halfway up. The crux comes toward the top. Use the great, rounded arête to finish.

7. Harlot (5.7) Climb the column and crack to the left side of the 3-foot ceiling. Protection is difficult because the crack is so wide. Climb onto the left face to avoid the mossy ceiling; this is the crux.

8. First Date (5.8) ✶ This route climbs the column on the right side of the 3-foot ceiling. The crux comes at the ceiling, which forces you onto the right-side face. The holds are small and mossy. On top of the big ledge, the route joins *Harlot*. Climb the column on the left, set back from the cliff.

9. Almost Pollock (5.8) ✶✶ Climb *Double Crack* for 30 feet. After passing the plant in the crack, step left and climb the crack and column to the ceiling's left side. The crux comes after the ceiling at a small bulge. The route protects well, except the last 30 feet. This section requires larger gear, up to 10 inches.

10. Double Crack (5.7) ✶✶ This fun route is tall but mossy. It protects well but requires large gear. The route is pretty sustained. The crux comes below the 2-foot ceiling. This route offers good stemming and jamming practice.

11. The Dime (5.9) ✶✶ The sharp, off-width crack at the top degrades the route. It protects well but takes large gear, up to 12 inches. For this reason, it makes a better toprope than lead. At the ceiling halfway up, step left and climb small face holds. The crux comes at the top section. The off-width crack requires arm bars, knee bars, and heel-toe jams.

12. Throw It Back (5.9) ✶ This is a great route, except for the off-width section and sharp rock. Climb for 30 feet to the pillar's top. The crux comes through the next 20 feet; the rock is mossy through this section. Both cracks are wide, so large gear is needed. The last 40 feet is great. It protects well with medium-size cams.

APPENDIX A: GLOSSARY

aid: means of getting up a climb using other than the actions of hands, feet, and body English.

aid climb: using equipment for direct assistance, which allows passage over rock otherwise impossible using only hands and feet; opposite of *free climb*.

Aliens: one type of spring-loaded camming device (SLCD), the most popular types of anchors. See also **Friends.**

anchor: a means by which climbers are secured to a cliff.

anchor matrix: the placement of anchors using various rigging systems.

arête: an outside edge or corner of rock, like the outer spine of a book, sometimes as large as a mountain ridge.

arm bar: a means of holding onto a wide crack; also called *arm lock*.

arm lock: see **arm bar.**

backstep: climbing move; placing the outside edge of the foot behind, (usually) on a vertical hold.

bashie: a piece of malleable metal that has been hammered into a rock seam as an anchor; used in extreme aid climbing.

belay: procedure of securing a climber by the use of a rope.

bi-doigt: a two-finger handhold.

Big Dudes: one type of spring-loaded camming device (SLCD), the most popular types of anchors. See also **Friends.**

big wall: a long climb traditionally done over multiple days, but which may take just a few hours for ace climbers. See also **wall.**

bight: a loop, as in a bight of rope.

biners: see **carabiners.**

bolt: an artificial anchor placed in a hole drilled for that purpose.

bomber: absolutely fail-safe (as in a very solid anchor or big, big handhold); sometimes called *bombproof.*

bombproof: see **bomber.**

bridging: see **stemming.**

bucket: a handhold large enough to fully latch onto, like the handle of a bucket.

buttress: an outside edge of rock that's much broader than an arête, definitely mountain-size.

cam: to lodge in a crack by counterpressure; that which lodges.

Camalots: one type of spring-loaded camming device (SLCD), the most popular types of anchors. See also **Friends.**

carabiners: aluminum alloy rings equipped with a spring-loaded snap gate; sometimes called *biners* or *krabs.*

ceiling: a section of rock that extends out above your head; an overhang of sufficient size to loom overhead; sometimes called *roof.*

chalk: standard equipment used to soak up finger and hand sweat on holds, although not allowed at certain areas.

chickenhead: a bulbous knob of rock.

chimney: a crack of sufficient size to accept an entire body.

chock: see **nut.**

chockstone: a rock lodged in a crack.

Class 1: mountain travel classification for trail hiking.

Class 2: mountain travel classification for hiking over rough ground, such as scree and talus; may include the use of hands for stability.

Class 3: mountain travel classification for scrambling that requires the use of hands and careful foot placement.

Class 4: mountain travel classification for scrambling over steep and exposed terrain; a rope may be used for safety on exposed areas.

Class 5: mountain travel classification for technical "free" climbing where terrain is steep and exposed, requiring the use of ropes, protection hardware, and related techniques. See also **Yosemite Decimal System (YDS).**

Class 6: mountain travel classification for aid climbing where climbing equipment is used for balance, rest, or progress; denoted with the letter A followed by numerals 0 to 5 (ex: 5.9/A3, meaning the free-climbing difficulties are up to 5.9 with an aid section of A3 difficulty).

clean: routes that are variously free of vegetation or loose rock, or where you don't need to place pitons; also the act of removing chocks and other gear from a pitch.

cling grip: a handhold where you grasp an edge with your fingers.

cold shut: a relatively soft metal ring that can be closed with a hammer blow; notoriously unreliable for withstanding high loads; commonly found as anchors atop short sport climbs.

cordelette: standard tackle that facilitates equalizing the load between two or more anchors; a 16-foot section of 6-mm Spectra is tied into a loop and clipped through all the anchor pieces, then tied off to create a single tie-in point, forming separate and equalized loops.

crack: type of irregularity on the stone.

crimper: a small but positive sharp edge.

crux: the most difficult section of a climb or pitch, typically marked on topos with the difficulty rating.

difficulty rating: see **Classes 1–6, Grades I–VI, R-rated climb, X-rated climb,** and **Yosemite Decimal System (YDS).**

dihedral: an inside corner of the climbing surface, formed by two planes of rock, like the oblique angle formed by the pages in an open book.

downclimb: a descent without rope, usually when rappelling is unsafe or impractical.

drag: used in reference to the resistance of rope running through carabiners.

dynamic: see **dyno** or **mo.**

dyno: lunge move; sometimes called *dynamic* or *mo.*

edge: a small hold ledge or the act of standing on an edge.

edging: climbing move; placing the very edge of the shoe on any hold that is clear-cut.

exposure: a relative situation where a climb has particularly noticeable sheerness.

flake: type of irregularity on the stone.

flag: using a limb as a counterbalance.

flash: free climbing a route from bottom to top on your first try.

footwork: the art and method of standing on holds.

free: see **free climb.**

free ascent: see **free climb.**

free climb: the upward progress gained by a climber's own efforts, using hands and feet on available features, unaided or free of attending ropes and gear. Rope is only used to safeguard against injury, not for upward progress or resting; opposite of *aid climb;* also called *free* or *free ascent.*

free solo: free climbing a route alone from bottom to top on your first try.

Friends: Spring-loaded camming devices (SLCDs) that can be used in all situations; the most popular type of anchors. These include Aliens, Big Dudes, Camalots, TCUs, and Quad Cams.

frog step: a climbing move where you bring one foot up, then the other, while keeping your torso at the same level, forming a crouched or "bullfrog" position.

gobies: hand abrasions.

grade: a rating that tells how much time an experienced climber will take on a given climb; the "overall seriousness" grade (referring to the level of commitment, overall technical difficulty, ease of escape, and length of route), denoted by Roman numerals.

Grade I: a climb that may take only a few hours to complete, such as Class 4 scrambles and Class 5 climbs.

Grade II: a climb that may take three to four hours.

Grade III: a climb that may take four to six hours, a strong half day.

Grade IV: a climb that may take a full day.

Grade V: a climb that may take one or two days and involve technical difficulties, weather, and other objective hazards, such as rockfall or avalanche danger; a bivouac is usually unavoidable.

Grade VI: a climb that may take two or more days on the wall.

greasy: adjective used to describe a slick surface.

hangdog: when a leader hangs from a piece of protection to rest, then continues on without lowering down; not a free ascent.

headwall: a much steeper section of cliff, residing toward the top.

heel hooking: the attempt to use the foot as a hand, usually on a vertical climb, where the heel is kicked over the head and hooked over a large hold.

hex: see **hexentric.**

hexentric: six-sided or barrel-shaped anchor that can be wedged into wide cracks and bottlenecks; sometimes called *hex.*

horn: a flakelike projection of rock, generally of small size.

jam: wedging feet, hands, fingers, or other body parts to gain purchase in a crack.

jugs: like a jug handle.

kneedrop: climbing move where the knee is dropped low and the rump is right over the foot.

krabs: see **carabiners.**

layback: see **lieback.**

lead: to be the first on a climb, belayed from below, and placing protection to safeguard a fall.

lieback: climbing maneuver that entails pulling with the hands while pushing with the feet; also called *layback.*

line: the path of the route, usually the line of least resistance between other major features of the rock.

mantle: climbing maneuver used to gain a single feature above your head.

mantleshelf: a rock feature, typically a ledge with scant holds directly above.

mantling: the act of surmounting a mantelshelf.

mo: see **dyno**.

mono-doigt: a one-finger handhold, as in "mono-doigt pockets."

move: movement; one of a series of motions necessary to gain climbing distance.

nut: a wedge or mechanical device that provides secure anchor to the rock; sometimes called a *chock.*

on-sight: to climb a route without prior knowledge or experience of the moves, without falling or otherwise weighting the rope (also called a *flash*).

open grip: a handhold where the edge or pocket supports your fingers out to the second joint (or farther) and your hand lies flat against the wall.

opposition: nuts, anchors, or climbing maneuvers that are held in place by the simultaneous stress of two forces working against each other.

"passive" nut: nonmechanical carabiner; see also **nut** and **carabiners.**

pegs: see **pitons.**

pinch grip: a handhold where the thumb pinches in opposition to the fingers on either side of a projection.

pinkpoint: to lead (without falling) a climb that has been preprotected with anchors rigged with carabiners.

pins: see **pitons.**

pitch: the section of rope between belays.

pitons: metal spikes of various shapes that are hammered into the rock to provide anchors in cracks; sometimes called *pins* or *pegs.* These types of anchors were common in the 1970s.

placement: the position of a nut or anchor.

pocket: a hole or cavity in the climbing surface used as a hold.

pocket pulling: an exhausting type of climb most often found on limestone, dolomite, and welded tuff formations.

pro: see **protection.**

problem: a boulder route.

project: a climb bolted but not yet redpointed.

protection: the anchors used to safeguard the leader; sometimes called *pro.* (Until the 1970s, protection devices were almost exclusively pitons—steel spikes that were hammered into cracks in the rock. Since then, various alloy wedges and intricate camming devices have virtually replaced pitons as generic protection devices. These wedges and cams are fitted into hollows and constrictions in cracks, and when fallen upon actually wedge farther into the rock. In the absence of cracks, permanent bolt anchors are drilled and fitted into the rock.)

prusik: both the knot and any means by which you mechanically ascend a rope.

pulling plastic: indoor wall climbing.

pumpy: adjective that indicates the continuous nature of the climb.

Quad Cams: one type of spring-loaded camming device (SLCD), the most popular types of anchors. See also **Friends.**

quickdraws: short slings with carabiners at both ends that help provide drag-free rope management for the leader.

rack: the collection of gear a climber takes up the climb.

rappel: to descend a rope by means of mechanical brake devices.

redpoint: to lead a route, clipping protection as you go, without falling or resting on protection.

rib: a narrow buttress, not as sharp as an arête.

ring grip: a handhold where fingers are nestled close together, with the thumb wrapped over the index finger.

roof: see **ceiling.**

RPs: small wired nuts used in aid climbing.

R-rated climb: protection or danger rating for climbs with serious injury potential; protection may be sparse or *runout,* or some placements may not hold a fall.

runner: see **sling.**

runout: the distance between two points of protection; often referring to a long stretch of climbing without protection.

sandbagging: the "shameful" practice of underestimating the actual difficulty of a given route. See also **"stiff" ratings.**

second: the second person on a rope team, usually the leader's belayer.

sidepull: pulling on a vertically aligned hold to the side of the body.

signals: a set of commands used between climber and belayer.

slab: a section of rock or gentle angle, sometimes a relative reference when it's a part of a vertical wall.

sling: a webbing loop used for a variety of purposes to anchor to the rock; used to sling gear on; sometimes called a *runner*.

smear, smearing: climbing move; standing on the front of the foot to gain friction against the rock across the breadth of the sole in order to adhere to the rock.

"soft" ratings: ratings deemed harder than the actual difficulty of a given route; opposite of *"stiff" ratings*.

Spectra: a popular climbing rope that's stronger than nylon; also called Spectra cord, Spectra line.

spring-loaded camming devices (SLCDs): see **Friends.**

spring step: a climbing move where you "bounce" off your foot to propel your weight upward.

stance: a standing rest spot, often the site of a belay.

static step: a climbing move where you press your weight on one leg while. simultaneously bringing your other foot up to the next hold; generally the most strenuous and least efficient way to move.

stemming: the process of counter-pressuring with the feet between two widely spaced holds; sometimes called *bridging*.

"stiff" ratings: ratings deemed easier than the actual difficulty of a given route; opposite of *"soft" ratings*. See also **sandbagging.**

stringing your nuts: attaching a length of rope to hexes and tapers rather than using a swaged cable.

Stoppers: original tapers made by Chouinard Equipment (now Black Diamond).

sustained: adjective that indicates the continuous nature of the climb.

taper: an anchor, typically in a boxy shape, that can vary from thumbnail-size micros to 1½-inch bombers. Variations follow four basic patterns: straight taper, curved taper, offset taper, and micro bass or micro steel taper.

TCUs: see **three-cam units.**

TDR: see **Thermo Dynamic Rubber.**

Thermo Dynamic Rubber (TDR): a petroleum-based synthetic product used for rubber-soled climbing shoes.

thin: a climb or hold of relatively featureless character.

three-cam units (TCUs): spring-loaded camming devices (SLCDs) designed specifically for thin cracks. See also **Friends.**

thrutch: To strain excessively; to move up, as in "Layback or thrutch up a low-angle chimney."

toeing-in: to edge with the shoe pointing straight on the hold; especially useful in small pockets.

toprope: a belay from an anchor point above; protects the climber from falling even a short distance.

traverse: to move sideways, without altitude gain.

tri-cam: an anchor that creates a tripod inside a crack or pocket.

undercling: grabbing a hold with the palm up, often used as a balancing tactic until a free hand can reach above to a better hold.

wall: a long climb traditionally done over multiple days, but which may take just a few hours for ace climbers. See also **big wall.**

work: refers to the expense of time and effort on numerous attempts to piece together the moves of a climb.

wrap: a handhold where the thumb is wrapped over a positive edge and the fingers are stacked on top of the thumb.

X-rated climb: protection or danger rating for climbs with ground-fall and death potential.

YDS: See Yosemite Decimal System.

Yosemite Decimal System (YDS): the usual American grading scale for identifying technical difficulty of routes, where 5 denotes the class and the numerals following the decimal point indicate the difficulty rating, usually according to the most difficult move. Subgrades (a, b, c, and d) are used on climbs rated 5.10 and harder. When the grade is uncertain, two letters may be used (ex: a/b), which is a finer comparison of technical difficulty than the more general plus and minus (+ and -) signs.

APPENDIX B:
AUTHORS' FAVORITE CLIMBS

Below are some of our favorite climbs, each with its own merits and attributes that makes it an excellent route. Those attributes may be rock quality, length, exposure, scenery, or simple enjoyment factor.

South Face (5.4, Santiam Pinnacle)
Hawaiian Slab (5.5, Spring Mountain)
Free Ride to Heaven (5.6, Anthony Lake)
The Americas (5.6, French's Dome)
Spiderman (5.7, Smith Rock)
Escalade (5.7, Pete's Pile)
Lime Ricky (5.7, Burnt River Canyon)
The Airy Traverse (5.7 R, The Steeple)
Zig Zag a Roof (5.7, Anthony Lake)
Jet Wind (5.8, Bulo Point)
Spacey Face (5.8 High Valley)
Out of Harm's Way (5.8, Smith Rock)
12 Minutes (5.9, Wolf Rock)
DaKind (5.9, Bulo Point)
Fret Arête (5.9, High Valley)
Jet Stream (5.9, Bulo Point)
Pumpin For the Man (5.9t, Pete's Pile)
The Outsiders (5.9, Smith Rock)
New Testament (5.10a, Smith Rock)
Dew, Chalk, and Blood (5.10a, Meadow Picnic Area)
Skinny Hippie (5.10a, Spring Mountain)
Silver Streak (5.10b, French's Dome)
Stairs to the Stars (5.10b, Wolf Rock)
Chicken Legs (5.11a, Lower Menagerie)
Jesus Saves (5.11a, Meadow Picnic Area)
Mojo Rising (5.11a, Spring Mountain)
Woman In the Meadow (5.11a, Smith Rock)
Ring of Fire (5.11d, Smith Rock)
The Flat Earth (5.12a/b, Smith Rock)
West Face (5.12a, C2, Smith Rock)

APPENDIX C:
SECONDARY DATA SOURCES

Secondary data sources are used to capture factual, public knowledge of route grades and names. In an effort to maintain consistency with historical public knowledge, where possible, route names and grades have been adopted from prepublished works or secondary data sources. Information taken from these sources is considered factual in nature and resides within the public domain as "common public knowledge."

Anglin, Jim. *Climbing Guide to the Menagerie Wilderness Area.* Self published. 1999.

Brown, Steve. E-mail interview with authors about High Valley and Burnt Valley route names and grades. September 2004.

DeLorme. *Oregon Atlas & Gazetteer.* 3rd ed. Yarmouth, ME: DeLorme, 1998.

Dodge, Nicholas A. *A Climbing Guide to Oregon.* Beaverton, OR: Touchstone Press, 1975.

Maps a la carte, Inc. *TopoZone.* http://www.topozone.com.

Olson, Tim. *Portland Rock Climbs.* Rev. ed. Chelsea, MI: Sheridan Books, 2001.

Orton, Greg. *Rock Climbing Southwest Oregon.* La Crescenta, CA: Mountain N' Air Books, 2001.

Pogue, Kevin. *Kevin Pogue's Climbing Page.* http://people.whitman.edu/%7Epogue/climbing.html (accessed February 2003).

Sullivan, William. *Exploring Oregon's Wild Areas.* 2nd ed. Seattle, WA: Mountaineers, 1994.

Toula, Tim. *Rock 'n Road.* Evergreen, CO: Chockstone Press, 1995.

Watts, Alan. *Climber's Guide to Smith Rock.* Evergreen, CO: Chockstone Press, 1992.

ROUTES BY RATING INDEX

This chart represents the number of documented climbs within each difficulty grade.

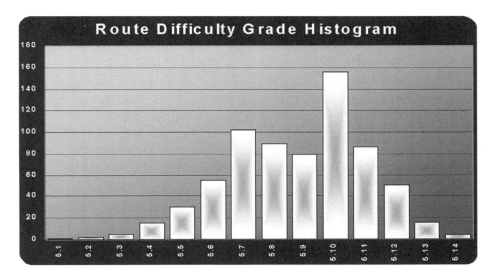

5.1
❏ *The Crawl* (Santiam Pinnacle), 158
❏ *SW Scramble* (Wolf Rock), 147

5.2
❏ *Front Gates 46* (Sisters Boulders), 182

5.3
❏ *Chucky Cheese* (Badlands), 249
❏ *Drive In 41* (Badlands), 253
❏ *Front Gates 8* (Sisters Boulders), 180
❏ *Front Gates 23* (Sisters Boulders), 181
❏ *Front Gates 40* (Sisters Boulders), 182

5.4
❏ *Beginner's Route* (Spring Mountain), 49
❏ *Drive In 10* (Badlands), 248
❏ *Drive In 34* (Badlands), 252
❏ *Drive In 49* (Badlands), 254

❏ *Drive In 50* (Badlands), 254
❏ *Eightball* (Badlands), 254
❏ *Elastic Crack* (Anthony Lake), 23
❏ *Front Gates 35* (Sisters Boulders), 181
❏ *God's Valley Chimney* (High Valley), 42
❏ *Left Slab Crack* (Smith Rock), 198
❏ *Pristine Christine* (Iron Wall), 164
❏ *Scott's Staircase* (Anthony Lake), 25
❏ *Solo Superstar* (Santiam Pinnacle), 160
❏ *South Face* (Santiam Pinnacle), 156
❏ *Wood Fur* (Bulo Point), 79

5.5
❏ *Bad Tendencies* (Highway 11), 125
❏ *Bowling Alley* (Smith Rock), 210
❏ *Cinnamon & Sugar* (Smith Rock), 198
❏ *Drive In 12* (Badlands), 248
❏ *Drive In 35* (Badlands), 252
❏ *East Fortress 52* (Sisters Boulders), 182

5.11d

- [ ] *Astro Monkey* (Smith Rock), 216
- [ ] *Billy Goat* (Smith Rock), 235
- [ ] *Cornerstone* (Smith Rock), 214
- [ ] *Drama Queen* (Spring Mountain), 63
- [ ] *Eggs Overhard* (Lower Menagerie), 135
- [ ] *Freddy's Dead* (Spring Mountain), 141
- [ ] *Front Gates 44* (Sisters Boulders), 182
- [ ] *Get a Grip* (Spring Mountain), 59
- [ ] *Iridescence* (Burnt River Canyon), 15
- [ ] *Mark's Route* (Spring Mountain), 60
- [ ] *Moonstone* (Meadow Picnic Area), 269
- [ ] *Moving In Stereo* (Smith Rock), 216
- [ ] *Rawhide* (Smith Rock), 206
- [ ] *Ring of Fire* (Smith Rock), 211
- [ ] *Rising Expectations* (Smith Rock), 218
- [ ] *Runaway Bunny* (Smith Rock), 233
- [ ] *Sunshine Dihedral* (Smith Rock), 202
- [ ] *Tick Spray* (Spring Mountain), 61
- [ ] *Time Warp* (Burnt River Canyon), 16
- [ ] *Unnamed* (Spring Mountain), 69
- [ ] *West Fortress 72* (Sisters Boulders), 184
- [ ] *Zebra Seam* (Smith Rock), 194

5.12a

- [ ] *Chubby Hubby* (Spring Mountain), 61
- [ ] *Death Takes a Holiday* (Smith Rock), 214
- [ ] *Dog Show* (Spring Mountain), 52
- [ ] *Double Pump* (La Pine Wall), 283
- [ ] *Drawin' a Blank* (Bulo Point), 78
- [ ] *Dreamin* (Smith Rock), 207
- [ ] *Elvis is Everywhere* (High Valley), 43
- [ ] *Hercules* (Meadow Picnic Area), 276
- [ ] *Latin Lover* (Smith Rock), 200
- [ ] *North Face* (Smith Rock), 217
- [ ] *Puppets Without Strings* (Spring Mountain), 63

- [ ] *Rad Ramp* (Meadow Picnic Area), 269
- [ ] *Randomly Focused Thoughts for Brief Periods of Time* (Smith Rock), 224
- [ ] *Risk Shy* (Smith Rock), 208
- [ ] *Smackdown* (Spring Mountain), 61
- [ ] *Spank the Monkey* (Smith Rock), 218
- [ ] *Take a Powder* (Smith Rock), 200
- [ ] *Torrid Zone* (Smith Rock), 236
- [ ] *Unnamed* (Spring Mountain), 49

5.12b

- [ ] *Boy Prophet* (Smith Rock), 207
- [ ] *Energy Crisis* (Smith Rock), 194
- [ ] *Latest Rage* (Smith Rock), 200
- [ ] *Peepshow* (Smith Rock), 200
- [ ] *Pump-O-Rama* (French's Dome), 106
- [ ] *Road Face* (French's Dome), 106
- [ ] *Sheer Trickery* (Smith Rock), 217
- [ ] *The Flat Earth* (Smith Rock), 202
- [ ] *Unnamed* (Spring Mountain), 62
- [ ] *Watts Tots* (Smith Rock), 200
- [ ] *West Fortress 88* (Sisters Boulders), 186

5.12c

- [ ] *Blister In The Sun* (Spring Mountain), 69
- [ ] *Chain Reaction* (Smith Rock), 203
- [ ] *Go Dog Go* (Smith Rock), 205
- [ ] *Heinous Cling* (Smith Rock), 203
- [ ] *High Voltage* (French's Dome), 106
- [ ] *Last Waltz* (Smith Rock), 202
- [ ] *Pose Down* (Smith Rock), 216
- [ ] *Powder In the Eyes* (Smith Rock), 202
- [ ] *Slopers* (La Pine Wall), 280
- [ ] *TNT* (Iron Wall), 168

5.12d

- [ ] *Choke On This* (Smith Rock), 206
- [ ] *I Am Not the Man* (Bulo Point), 81

INDEX

Front Gates 46 (Sisters Boulders), 182
Full of Campers (Sisters Boulders), 184
Fundamental Physics (Sisters Boulders), 184
Funny Trumpets Arête (Spring Mountain), 54

G

Genesis (Youtlkut Pillars), 300
Get a Grip (Spring Mountain), 59
Get Up Stand Up (Wolf Rock), 153
Giant's Staircase (French's Dome), 110
Gidrah (Spring Mountain), 64
Ginger Snap (Smith Rock), 198
Go Dog Go (Smith Rock), 205
Go Gonzo (Santiam Pinnacle), 160
God's Valley Chimney (High Valley), 42
Go-Go-Go (Crack in the Ground), 291
Golgotha (Smith Rock), 208
Gome Boy (Spring Mountain), 49
Good-N-Plenty (Badlands), 250
Gork (Crack in the Ground), 292
Grandma's House (Smith Rock), 227
Grass Stain (Sisters Boulders), 180
Green Ridge, 169
Guillotine (Pete's Pile), 95
Gumby (Smith Rock), 195

H

Hammer Time (Sisters Boulders), 180
Handyman (Smith Rock), 227
Hang 'em Higher (Spring Mountain), 62
Hang It Loose (Smith Rock), 235
Happy Dog (Crack in the Ground), 292
Happy Man (Meadow Picnic Area), 269
Hard One (Badlands), 255
Harlan Wall, 117
Harlot (Youtlkut Pillars), 301
Have Faith (Crack in the Ground), 290
Hawaiian Slab (Spring Mountain), 54

Headstone (Smith Rock), 236
Heinous Cling (Smith Rock), 203
Helium Woman (Smith Rock), 204
Hercules (Meadow Picnic Area), 276
Heresy (Smith Rock), 208
Hesitation Blues (Smith Rock), 211
High on Pockets (Sisters Boulders), 184
High Valley, 36
High Voltage (French's Dome), 106
Highway 11, 122
Hit This (Badlands), 252
Homer's Flake (Meadow Picnic Area), 270
Hop On Pop (Smith Rock), 197
Hospital Corner (Spring Mountain), 63
Hot For Teacher (Pete's Pile), 99
Hot Pockets (Badlands), 249

I

I Am Not the Man (Bulo Point), 81
If Clips Could Kill (Burnt River Canyon), 18
If I Ran the Circus (Smith Rock), 233
If Six Were Nine (Smith Rock), 225
In Harm's Way (Smith Rock), 213
Initiation (Spring Mountain), 58
Insomnia (High Valley), 43
Inspector Fuzz (Smith Rock), 236
Inversion Excursion (Bulo Point), 77
Iridescence (Burnt River Canyon), 15
Iron Gland (Iron Wall), 165
Iron Wall, 161
Irreverence (Smith Rock), 208

J

Jack and Jill (Spring Mountain), 49
Jammin (Sisters Boulders), 184
Jersey Shore (Smith Rock), 231

ABOUT THE AUTHORS

Adam Bolf

A native Oregonian, Adam Bolf started his technical climbing career in 1990 and has sent more than 1,100 different routes, including a number of difficult routes up the Cascades' tallest peaks. A graduate of the University of Phoenix with a bachelor's degree in business management, he is a program manager for a high-tech corporation and lives in Albany, Oregon. He spends his free time climbing, bicycling, and hiking with his wife, children, friends, and family. He and his wife, Christine, have spent months exploring the western United States and have climbed in more than seventy different locations in thirteen states.

Benjamin Ruef

An avid rock and mountain climber, Benjamin Ruef learned to climb at a young age from his father, a senior member of the Corvallis Mountain Rescue Unit. A native Oregonian, Benjamin has climbed throughout the United States, Europe, and Asia, and has ascended more than 1,000 different routes. He graduated from Oregon State University with a bachelor's degree in international business and completed an international business program at Agder University in Norway. He then spent a year living and working in South Korea as an English teacher. He currently lives in Oregon and works as financial analyst for the state.

ACCESS: IT'S EVERYONE'S CONCERN

The Access Fund is a national nonprofit climbers' organization working to keep climbing areas open and conserve the climbing environment. Need help with a climbing related issue? Call us and please consider these principles when climbing.

- **ASPIRE TO CLIMB WITHOUT LEAVING A TRACE:** Especially in environmentally sensitive areas like caves. Chalk can be a significant impact. Pick up litter and leave trees and plants intact.
- **MAINTAIN A LOW PROFILE:** Minimize noise and yelling at the crag.
- **DISPOSE OF HUMAN WASTE PROPERLY:** Use toilets whenever possible. If toilets are not available, dig a "cat hole" at least six inches deep and 200 feet from any water, trails, campsites or the base of climbs. Always pack out toilet paper. Use a "poop tube" on big wall routes.
- **USE EXISTING TRAILS:** Cutting switchbacks causes erosion. When walking off-trail, tread lightly, especially in the desert on cryptogamic soils.
- **BE DISCRETE WITH FIXED ANCHORS:** Bolts are controversial and are not a convenience. Avoid placing unless they are absolutely necessary. Camouflage all anchors and remove unsightly slings from rappel stations.
- **RESPECT THE RULES:** Speak up when other climbers do not. Expect restrictions in designated wilderness areas, rock art sites and caves. Power drills are illegal in wilderness and all national parks.
- **PARK AND CAMP IN DESIGNATED AREAS:** Some climbing areas require a permit for overnight camping.
- **RESPECT PRIVATE PROPERTY:** Be courteous to landowners.
- **JOIN THE ACCESS FUND:** To become a member, make a tax-deductible donation of $35.

P.O. Box 17010
Boulder, CO 80308
303.545.6772

ACCESS FUND
your climbing future
www.accessfund.org